Impacting on Recreation and Park Legislation

edited by

Daniel D. McLean

Cedar Rapids, Iowa Recreation Department

S. Harold Smith

Department of Recreation Management and Youth Leadership
Brigham Young University

ISBN 0-88314-476-X

Purposes of the American Alliance For Health, Physical Education, Recreation and Dance

The American Alliance is an educational organization, structured for the purposes of supporting, encouraging, and providing assistance to member groups and their personnel throughout the nation as they seek to initiate, develop, and conduct programs in health, leisure, and movement-related activities for the enrichment of human life.

Alliance objectives include:

1. Professional growth and development--to support, encourage, and provide guidance in the development and conduct of programs in health, leisure, and movement-related activities which are based on the needs, interests, and inherent capacities of the individual in today's society.

2. Communication--to facilitate public and professional understanding and appreciation of the importance and value of health, leisure, and movement-related activities as they contribute toward human well-being.

3. Research--to encourage and facilitate research which will enrich the depth and scope of health, leisure, and movement-related activities; and to disseminate the findings to the profession and other interested and concerned publics.

4. Standards and guidelines--to further the continuous development and evaluation of standards within the profession for personnel and programs in health, leisure, and movement-related activities.

5. Public affairs--to coordinate and administer a planned program of professional, public, and governmental relations that will improve education in areas of health, leisure, and movement-related activities.

6. To conduct such other activities as shall be approved by the Board of Governors and the Alliance Assembly, provided that the Alliance shall not engage in any activity which would be inconsistent with the status of an educational and charitable organization as defined in Section 501(c) (3) of the Internal Revenue Code of 1954 or any successor provision thereto, and none of the said purposes shall at any time be deemed or construed to be purposes other than the public benefit purposes and objectives consistent with such educational and charitable status.

HOW TO USE THIS PACKET

Recreation and Parks belong to the public. Decisions about funding, staffing, services, and facilities are shaped in the political arena. *Impacting on Recreation and Park Legislation* is a guide for changing public opinion concerning recreation and parks. It is written for those who have the courage and desire to influence the political decisions which affect the future of recreation and parks for our nation.

No two states are alike. No two communities have the same problems--nor the same resources. There is no single prescription for success. But, there are commonalties among the political environments, structures, and interventions which can change park and recreation policy.

Shaping political decisions successfully requires more than motivation. It requires a knowledge of the political process and a grasp of the tools that help sway decision-making.

Our government reflects the changing values, beliefs and needs of the public. Change is the only certainty. We can be a part of a changing world.

Impacting on Recreation and Park Legislation is divided into five sections for easy reference. Not everyone will need all of the information presented here, but rather may pick and choose the most pertinent and applicable sections. The book is intended as a resource manual--but it is mostly intended to be used.

Section II--Setting the Stage tells how the various levels of government are organized to provide support to recreation and parks, and the processes which turn public opinion into public policy. A brief history and some future trends concerning federal, state, and local role in funding recreation and parks is given. Also included is an explanation of the structure and function of the state legislatures and their relationship to state and local recreation and park policy.

Section III--Getting Started provides a model for mounting a comprehensive state wide legislative campaign. it suggests planning strategies and ways to involve people for successful political action.

Section IV--Tools of the Trade provides tools for action. It outlines techniques to educate voters and politicians, and giving samples.

Section V--Research and Resources offers questions and answers about recreation and parks, research excerpts, and support statements to help sell recreation and parks to political decision makers.

Table of Contents

1

Making Public Policy In a Federalist System

People who want to influence public policy face a variety of conflicts. They need to know what they can do. They might wonder if influencing the government is wrong. Citizens will want to know how they can interact with government in a legitimate way with some degree of intelligence, effectiveness and focus.

Our Government is based on the federalist model, which is a series of governments, each with its own role and jurisdiction. A helpful way to look at our governing forces is to use the Public Policy Making Grid (Figure 1.1). This grid shows the three levels of government--federal, state, and local--and the three branches of government--executive, legislative, and judicial--in a matrix. This is a clear way of viewing the dividing lines of government power.

Public Policy

Public policy can be defined as the expression of policy by the government, which reflects the common philosophies, values and desires of its citizens. To influence public policy, find out which government structure has jurisdiction over an issue. A local legislative issue is a matter for the city council. A state executive issue might be a matter for the state director of natural resources. A national judicial issue could be a coalition of conservation groups suing to prevent administrative changes in the management of the National Wilderness System. The first step in influencing public policy is to place an issue on the grid.

The Three Branches

The framers of the Constitution meant to provide a stable government that would protect property against the leveling tendencies of the majority. They created the electoral college and a powerful judiciary, and provided for the indirect election of senators through the state legislatures.

The early leaders designed a system of three branches of government: executive, legislative, and judicial. Developed as a check and balance on the excessive use of power, the three branches were a reaction against the tyranny of the British monarch. In simple terms, the legislative branch makes the law; the judicial branch administers it; and the judicial to adjudicates it. Each defines the way government relates to citizens.

Executive

Although laws are made by the legislative branch, legislation is not the only way to make public policy. The executive branch can make policy in the ways it chooses to administer the laws set down by the legislative branch. For instance, when Congress passed the initial legislation requiring environmental impact statements for projects, it intended the agency to prepare a two to three page document. The executive branch interpreted a much broader meaning, resulting in today's multimillion dollar environmental impact statements by all levels of the public and private sector.

Within the executive branch is a myriad of public officials, who each have responsibility for some decision making. Collectively, these decisions express the public policy of the executive branch, a policy which changes with each administration, because the chief executive and his policies govern at the direct request of the people. The newly elected executive represents the policies that the people have said they want. A good government bureaucrat whose tenure transcends any administration, reflects the views and policies of the administration currently in power.

Citizens express their opinions to the executive branch primarily by electing the chief executive-- the president, the governor, or the mayor. As our system of government has become more complicated, other mechanisms for public input, such as public hearings or public comment, have become more formalized. All federal regulations are subject to public comment. Many state policy decisions are preceded by regional hearings designed to garner input from professional providers and consumers of relevant state services. Volatile political issues are often handled this way to diffuse public outcry and to move the decision to the most politically expedient or publicly accepted middle ground.

Public Policy Making Grid			
	EXECUTIVE	LEGISLATIVE	JUDICIAL
FEDERAL	President, Vice Pesident, Cabinet, Federal Agencies, Presidential Councils, etc.	U.S. Congress, Congressional Budget Office, Library of Congress, other Congressional Offices	Supreme Court, Federal Court System
STATE	Governor, Cabinet, State Agencies, Special Commissions, and Councils,	State Legislature, State Legislative Offices	State Supreme Court, State Court System
LOCAL	Mayor, City/Town Offices	City/Town Council, Board of Supervisors*	Local Court System

*Local Governments are defined by state law. In some counties, the chairman of the board of supervisors functions as a chief executive.

Figure 1.1 Public Policy Making Grid

Legislative

The legislative branch is the easiest to influence, and the one most directly responsible to the people. Legislators are elected from specific geographic districts, and represent fewer people than the executive branch.

Citizens express their needs to the legislature in a variety of ways, primarily by voting for their legislators and participating in their party campaigns at the local level. Other common ways to influence legislative policy are by writing letters to legislators or testifying at public hearings. Hearings are usually held in conjunction with proposed new legislation, the budget and appropriations process, and oversight activities. The legislature can hold hearings on almost anything that could be considered "public business."

Judicial

The judicial branch was designed as the most distant from public influence. The function of the judicial branch is to ensure that laws are consistent with the Constitution and that the administration of the law is consistent with its language or intent.

Although some judges are elected, they are usually appointed and have stringent guidelines for removal from office. The intent was to make them more impervious to the political whims which affect the legislative and executive branches, but court decisions remain an expression of public policy.

Because individuals can have an impact on the judicial system only by filing suit, the judicial system is seen as largely responsive, taking little initiative of its own. It responds to complaints from the citizens about the constitutionality, interpretation, or administration of a law. Another common way to interact with the judicial system is to file as a friend of the court, or to file as part of a class action, which means that the decision would apply to an entire class of people, such as children under 18 in a particular state, or women, etc

The Three Levels

Although the concepts of democracy and equality upon which our country was founded solidified slowly, the desire for independence was always pervasive. The very name of our country, the United States, reflects our paradoxical desire to be independent states, yet united and strong. The early leaders of our country took various positions on this continuum of independence--unity. They saw the advantage of a strong central government as crucial to the survival of our new nation. With the election of Thomas Jefferson, however, the concept of decentralization took hold. Jefferson wanted a majority of the power to be centered in local governments, and advocated for New England style town meetings. Jefferson is credited with what became the concept of states' rights.

Unlike the three branches of government, the roles of the three levels of government throughout our history have been less clearly defined. The very obvious role for the federal government is national issues. The states have traditionally been concerned with the health and welfare of citizens. Local government tends to more immediate issues of zoning, property use, and local recreation and parks opportunities.

Power Shifts

During Franklin Roosevelt's term, the federal government began to take on new responsibilities. Job programs were developed, and food programs began. During the 1960s and the 1970s, the federal government began to increase its role with the Great Society and the War on Poverty. Federal programs were expanded and some programs were funded directly to local governments, bypassing the states altogether. Civil rights became an issue, and state and local governments came to be perceived as incapable or unwilling to guarantee basic constitutional rights. The federal government had to assume more authority to uphold the constitution.

President Reagan's "new federalism" program tried to shift some of the power which now rests with the federal government to the states and localities. President Reagan's "new federalism" was much the same as Thomas Jefferson's original notion, of "old federalism." The conflict over which level of government should appropriately have authority for a variety of areas is as old as our country itself. Just as the ideas of a perfect form of government were debated in the early days of our country, they are debated today. Some of the old arguments continue to haunt us.

America has been described as a welfare state by some government leaders and observers. The aging of the American population is changing the way government does and will continue to provide service. During the Reagan administration America experienced the largest deficits in history. In 1989, 14 % of the federal budget was allocated to debt payment. This is larger than the combined budgets of the Departments of Agriculture, Commerce, Education, Energy, Interior, Justice, Labor, State, and Transportation.

When discussing ways of influencing governments, it is generally helpful to look at which branch of government has the decision making power. In general, the closer the decision is to the people, the more personal the politics become. Although citizens may not personally know a United States Senator, they may very well know their state senator. In a small town, the mayor may be a close friend. This can both complicate and enhance the effectiveness of a lobbying effort. In general, because they are more visible, state and local governments are less forgiving. Conversely, a positive reputation, is generally more lasting and valuable on this level in the long run. Care, consistency, and credibility are extremely important.[1]

Public Policy For Recreation and Parks

The first and most pervasive truth about government is that it is subject to change. It is a dynamic system which is influenced by outside forces--economic situations, wars, politics and public sentiment. Likewise, today's government is not the past governments. Tomorrow's government will not be the government of today. Times change. Power shifts. The changing nature of our government enables citizens to have a hand in developing the future, but it blurs the boundaries of the Public Policy Making Grid, necessitating a more skillful and savvy approach. It can be very much like hitting a moving target. Committed, energetic people who are willing to learn as they go can have a hand in shaping public policy. Make public policy work for recreation and parks.

---

[1] Portions reprinted from the *Journal of Physical Education, Recreation and Dance*, September, 1983. Used with permission.

2

Recreation: Who is in Charge?

Historical Context

The U.S. Constitution makes no provision for recreation and parks, which from the earliest United States history were perceived as state, county, and municipal responsibilities. The park movement came to America with the early colonists. The park ideal had been developed in Europe and become a part of the fabric of society in larger European cities. As early as 1634, Boston Commons was an important part of the Boston community and Washington, D.C. represented the first major attempt to establish an American city with the garden park concept as a principal feature. New York City's Central Park, initiated in 1858, is credited with being the first American park designed for the public.

The recreation movement is often credited with its beginnings in the Boston Sand Gardens in 1885. The movement was an outgrowth of community recognition of the need to provide services for youth. By 1889, there were 21 playgrounds in Boston and, in 1893, a general superintendent was hired.

The recreation and park movement had begun. Communities all across America were inspired by Central Park. The large urban park became a model for many communities to emulate. Cities began to develop park systems and establish park departments. The 1880s and 1890s also saw the growth of community centers in large communities. Following the example of the development and broadening of the playground movement, settlement houses began to expand their activities to include more programs and become a gathering place for the community.

While communities recognized and established their roles as primary providers of recreation and parks, the states became actively involved in the park movement. The federal government had deeded Yosemite Valley to California in 1864, effectively creating the first state park. The park was not maintained and ultimately returned to the federal government. New York created the first recognized state park in 1899. The Adirondack State Park signaled the birth of state park systems. In 1917, the Illinois Division of Parks and Monuments was established as the first state level department. Yellowstone, carved out of the Wyoming wilderness, was established as the world's first national park in 1872. This was the first acknowledgment by the federal government of the need to provide preservation for unique natural resources at the federal level. Another 44 years passed before congress established a system to manage the national park system. The White House recognized the importance of outdoor recreation and, in 1924, sponsored the first "White House Conference on Outdoor Recreation." Subsequent national reports followed in 1962, 1973, and 1986.

Each level of government has carved out its role in the recreation and park movement. Figure 2.1 illustrates the relationships present at each of the three levels of government and the role of the courts in the process. The federal government has been, until recently, concerned exclusively with resource protection through the National Park Service, and multiple resource management through the U.S. Forest Service, Bureau of Land Management, Army Corps of Engineers, and Bureau of Reclamation. States have been primarily concerned with natural resource acquisition and management and the provision of park systems. Counties, dependent upon their proximity to urban areas, have had a mixed role in the provision of recreation and park resources and services. The more urban the area, the more apt the organization is to provide traditional municipal recreation programs in addition to natural

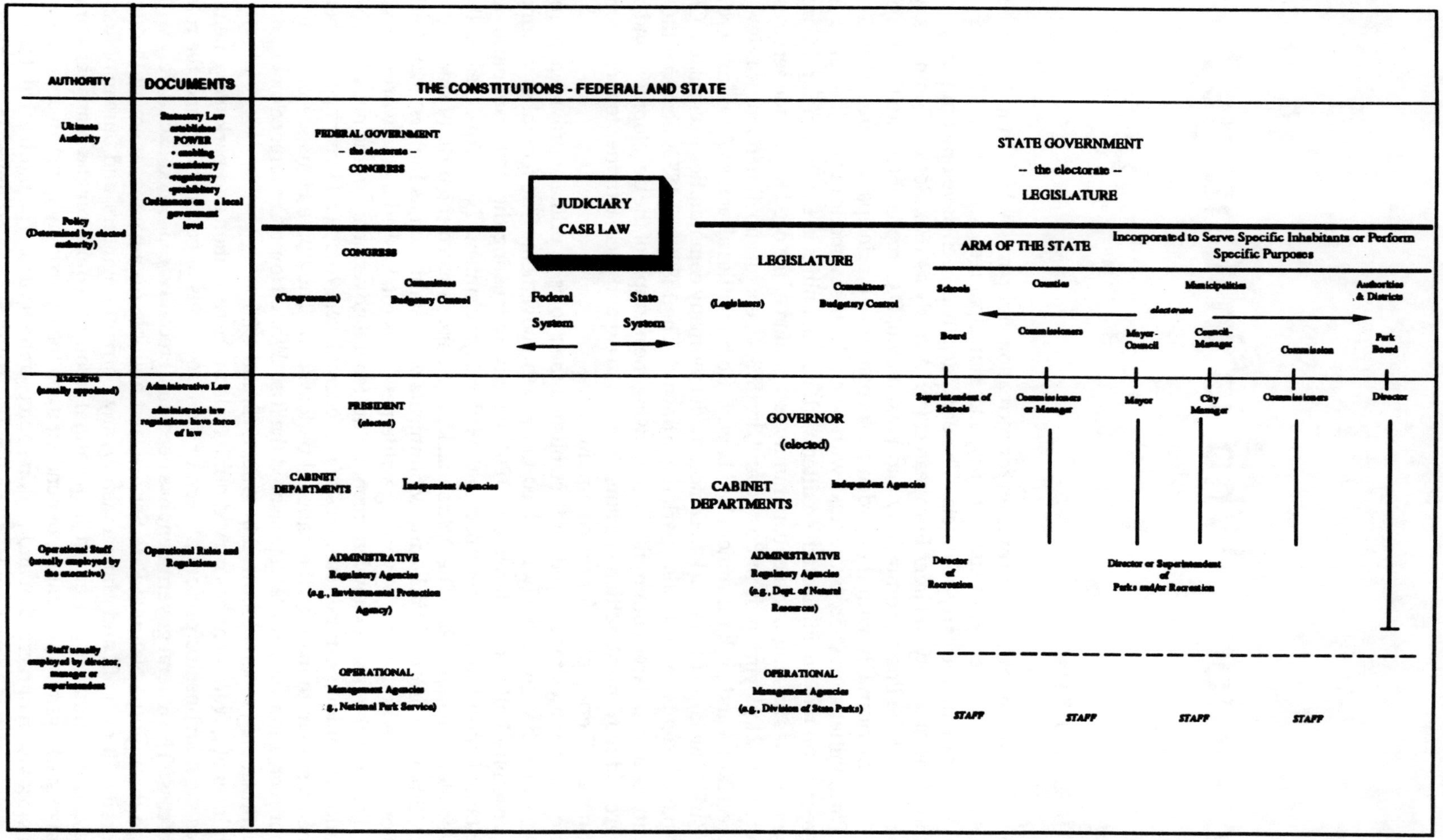

Figure 2.1: Roles of Government

areas and parks. Conversely, the more rural the location, the less likely the organization will be to provide traditional recreation services. A rural organization is more apt to concentrate on resource development and management. There are exceptions to each of these levels of service.

Municipalities have been the innovators in the recreation movement, providing important levels of service at the community level. As the movement gained momentum and acceptance, the various levels of government undertook roles that appeared to be a natural separation of responsibilities. Figure 2.2 shows government levels and the type of services each most frequently offers.

Recreation and Park Levels of Service		
LEVEL OF GOVERNMENT	RESOURCES PROVIDED	PROGRAM LEVEL
Federal Government National Park Service U.S. Forest Service Bureau of Land Management	National Parks Urban Parks National Monuments Wilderness Areas Forest Recreation Areas Wilderness Areas Recreation Areas Wilderness Areas Reservoirs Recreation Areas	Interpretation Resource Based Programming
Bureau of Reclamation & Corps of Engineers	State Parks State Recreation Areas	
State Government	County Parks Large Urban Parks	
County Government	Urban Park Systems Recreation Systems	Interpretation Resource Based Recreation

Figure 2.2 Recreation and Park Levels of Service

The Role of the States

The role of the states has been important in defining and legitimizing the recreation and park movement. State executive and legislative branches are involved in different roles as they deal with the local sector. States have traditionally provided:
- enabling legislation that authorizes the establishment of state, county, and municipal recreation and park systems (legislative branch);
- supervision and control of state park and resource systems (executive branch);
- financial support for state, county, and municipal recreation and park systems (appropriations--legislative branch; administration--executive branch).

State Legislatures

State legislatures enact laws to create and maintain state recreation and park systems. Laws enacted generally specify which organization of the branch of government is responsible for overseeing a park system. In each of the 50 states varying organizational structures exist. There has been a trend to combine the agencies involved in managing the state park system with other conservation related agencies at the state level (i.e, Department of Natural Resources).

State laws, created by the legislature, establish enabling legislation for county and municipal park systems. Legislation may allow school districts, municipal and county governments, or separate taxing districts to be created for these purposes. A wide variety of legislation exists in the various states. Some states have consolidated existing legislation while others seem to have enacted new legislation every time a unit of government wanted to do something different.

State legislatures also keep an eagle eye on their laws long after they have passed both houses. For the most part, the governor and the executive branch administer and regulate laws which the legislature passes. However, legislatures may also ensure that the letter and intent of the law is respected when it is administered. Like Congress, state legislatures may hold oversight hearings on any statute in danger of being administered in a manner inconsistent with the letter and intent of the law. In the past, state legislatures have used their oversight powers reluctantly, but there is a growing trend among legislatures to affirm their independence of the executive branch by exercising more authority over legislative mandates.

State legislatures also often have legislative review authority over executive branch regulations. Thirty-six states retain some mechanism to review regulations. Whereas law sets forth the action, rules or regulations explain how the public can expect to relate to the law. Congress and state legislatures occasionally accuse the executive branch of exceeding its powers and "making law" by writing regulations which stray too far from the legislation. In fact, legislation is sometimes intentionally vague for political reasons. If all relationships were detailed and clarified, the law might not have satisfied all parties as a good "compromise" piece of legislation. Because laws are often vague, and require executive branch clarification, various state administrative department officials and board members can have tremendous impact on the way a law finally relates to the public.

The State Executive Branch

All states have at least one agency that is responsible for parks and/or recreation. This agency's title varies from state to state. Some states have advisory boards. Others have none. Advisory boards, almost without exception, are appointed by the Governor and may or may not be ratified by the Senate.

The state executive branch is responsible for administration of the state park system in most states. In some states this role has expanded, and offices of recreation have been established for the purpose of working with other state agencies to provide services to county and municipal agencies, and to provide technical and research assistance. Other states have attempted to address public demand and pressures for increased revenue through innovation, such as the establishment of resorts, lodges, and meeting facilities as integral parts of the park system. New York state has established a center for recreation and sport research. The emphasis at the state level, however, remains upon conservation, preservation, and interpretation.

The executive branch has control over state allocated funds as well as the state portion of the Land and Water Conservation Fund. States administer funds using a variety of formulas.

Local Role

Local political systems vary even more than state systems. The U.S. Constitution's Tenth Amendment says that all powers not conferred on the federal government are "reserved" to the states. No mention is made of local governing units which exist by authority of the states. Except for those who live in unincorporated rural areas, most people live under the jurisdiction of both a municipal and a county government. The several forms local government may take–counties, towns, townships, cities, villages–vary considerably from state to state.

Counties

Traditionally, counties have been larger, often rural political subdivisions. Governed by a board of supervisors or commissioners which often serves as both the legislative and the executive branch, the county may be run by an elected or board appointed administrator. When elected by the people, the county executive assumes the function of the executive branch.

Counties play a major role in the provision of close to home outdoor recreation resources. Most often county park systems are seen as the intermediate system between the highly developed city parks and the less developed state parks. Dependent upon nearness to urban areas, county systems provide high-use urban park areas to remote, wilderness type settings. The emphasis is upon resources and instead of programs. In recent years the move towards more recreation programming and interpretation has increased, especially for those counties in close proximity to urban areas.

Municipalities

All municipal governments are elected by the people. The provision of recreation and parks is seen as one of the primary duties of these local governments. The level and type of service varies from community to community and is often based on size of the municipality.

Recreation and park departments, whether combined or separate, take two basic forms. Some are organized as part of the municipal government and are included in the municipal budget. Others are organized as separate districts with taxing power. The latter is most common in Illinois and in parts of California. Another form beginning to emerge in some areas of the nation, most notably California, contracts with private firms to provide recreation opportunities and to maintain park resources.

Influencing Public Policy

To influence public policy, find out which governmental or administrative unit has responsibility for policy decisions, such as a state recreation and park fund allocation decision. The state legislature either establishes the decision making process for the fund or they give that authority to the state natural resource agency, the state director, or to some other agency in state government. The policy can be reflected in state law, in regulations, or in administrative policies. In general, the closer decision making is to the people, the easier it is to influence decisions. In other words, it is probably easier to affect the local city council than the state natural resource board. The closer the administrative unit is to the voters, the easier it is for them to be heard. A decision maker whose job depends on the good will of the voters is more likely to listen to them. An elected city council member is more likely to listen to comments than an appointed recreation and park board member. By the same token, a county park board which serves a larger region and is somewhat removed from the local governing unit, is likely to be less responsive than a local recreation and park board.

Advisory Boards

Another mechanism for voicing public opinion and concern about public policies is the advisory board. Many state, district, county,and municipal governing units have advisory boards, or ad hoc boards that hear public opinion on a particular issue. Often state or federal laws require public input through such a process. Sometimes membership is mandated by legislation or administrative rules. Designated membership ensures that both primary and secondary consumers of a service are a part of the decision making.

In general, advisory boards have no direct decision making power, and they sometimes present the illusion of public input, while other politically expedient decisions are made. Just as often, they can forcefully influence decision making and win their points. The political see-saw doesn't always move in predictable rhythms. What often counts in such potential political conflicts is the unity and respect of board members. When their recommendations are taken seriously, they provide an additional mechanism for public input which should not be ignored.

Recreation and Park Funding

Public funding is a reflection of public values, and hence of public policy. It expresses where the public, through government officials, chooses to put their money. Public recreation and parks are financed with public dollars, and decisions about how and where these dollars are spent have always been controversial.

Although sufficient money does not guarantee a quality recreation and park system and services, it is hard to have good resources without money. In the past, public recreation and parks have been financed almost exclusively by local property taxes. More recently, however, public recreation and parks have had to be much more creative to secure adequate funding. Most departments depend heavily on revenues generated through their program and facility offerings to offset the cost of operations. Alternative funding sources are becoming more commonplace as municipal agencies attempt to overcome restricted growth or declining budgets.

Recent Trends

Just as states were beginning in the early to mid 1980s to search for additional funding sources for their many responsibilities, the pubic financial picture at all levels of government became bleak. A severe recession decreased business and corporate taxes, caused layoffs, and subsequently decreased sales, income, and property taxes. At the same time, the recession increased the need for public services and direct financial assistance, such as food stamps, unemployment, and welfare payments.

As of 1984, the economy began to recover, albeit at different paces throughout the country. State economies began to receive increased state revenues. Funding sources remained a major issue, but in a recovering economy with record revenues states were less willing to increase taxes, in view of the changes in the federal tax law that affected all Americans.

Funding for recreation and parks increased at the state and local level, but decreased under the Reagan administration at the federal level. The Land and Water Conservation fund went from a high of $390 million in 1977, of which $175.5 million went to state and local governments, to $202 million in 1989, of which only $20 million was allocated for state assistance. The Urban Park and Recreation Recovery Act, initiated with high hopes under the Carter administration, was reduced to zero funding during the Reagan years.

The Changing Federal Role

Since Franklin Roosevelt's administration the federal government has played an increasing role in domestic programs. Federal program growth was spurred by certain "categories" of issues perceived as needing national assistance. This stronger federal role emerged because of
- issues which crossed state lines;
- failure to serve certain groups of people;
- disproportionate concentrations of poor people in certain states and urban areas.

In addition to an increase in federal domestic programs, the 1960s and 1970s ushered in a new twist in funding dispersal. A direct line from federal to local governments or special districts was created. Federal funds often flow directly to a nonprofit agency or local goverment that administers a program, bypassing the state government entirely. As more regulations or "strings" were tied to federal funds, states began to feel a loss of power and control. They resented what some referred to as federal fiscal blackmail.

The 1980s brought the introduction of "New Federalism," and a professed desire on the part of President Reagan "to provide for greater authority and responsibility in the states, counties, and towns to return government to those closest to the people most affected."
President Reagan's March, 1980 budget request (for FY1981), proposed the following policy shifts:
- consolidation of 90 categorical programs into five block grants to the states;
- transfer of some authority from the federal government to the state;
- reduction in federal regulations and "strings" attached to federal funds; and
- across-the-board reduction of funds by 25 percent.
Congress responded by modifying and partially granting Reagan's request.

In reality, new federalism initiated elimination or major reductions of whole programs on which state and local governments had come to depend. Federal Revenue Sharing returned $4 billion to local government when it was eliminated in 1986. The Urban Development Action grants, trimmed in 1988, provided $675 million when they peaked. Almost $1 billion has been trimmed from the Community Development Block Grant program in 8 years. Environmental Protection Agency (EPA) grants have been cut by more than half (from $4.9 billion in 1980 to $2.3 billion in 1988). In addition, the 1986 Tax Reform Act provisions severely limited local governments' access to capital markets. In 1987, the first full year after the Tax Reform Act, the National League of Cities (NLC) reported there was a 34 % reduction in municipal bond issuance. Nearly 45 % of the cities surveyed by the NLC reported they had to reduce their capital budgets because of law changes. Losses of these programs proved traumatic for many recreation and park agencies. Increased regulations without appropriate funding continued to come from the federal level.

Issues for the 1990s

Because public funding is one of the most important ways to demonstrate public priorities, the recreation and park priorities of the 1990s will be reflected in how and where public money is used. The issues facing recreation and parks in the 1990s vary from region of the country to level of government. At the federal level, elimination of the Heritage Conservation and Recreation Service in the early 1980s was a severe set back for all levels of government. It signaled a step back from the forefront of leadership by the federal government. The elimination or virtual elimination of many supporting funds from the federal level placed increased stress on state, county, and local governments at a time when revenues were declining. The President's Commission on American's Outdoors, established by Presidential Proclamation in 1985, was one of the bright spots for recreation and parks in the 1980s. The final report was delivered to President Reagan in January 1987. The report has stirred much debate in and out of the administration.

The American public has witnessed a profound change in the way all governments do business during the 1980s. The trend to conservatism could continue into the 1990s. New federalism might continue under the post-Reagan years or perhaps a Democratically controlled congress will assert itself and make a new agenda for America. Several issues face all levels of government during the 1990s.

Financing Recreation and Parks

As indicated, the federal commitment to providing funds and resources to state and local governments has declined significantly. As John Herbers, in Governing States and Localities stated of the Reagan era, "Although the states and localities have emerged from the Reagan era strengthened, more independent and as the source of innovations, the pressures under which they operate may well be more severe and numerous than those of the past 8 years." [2] Sources of state and local funding must increase significantly in the next decade. Local and state leaders must find new methods to finance recreation and parks. Methods must be innovative but must not place additional burdens upon revolt minded tax payers. If states and localities persist in relying on property and income taxes for recreation and parks funding, there will be little or no growth. Local leaders must work with state legislatures to change tax and finance laws to ensure greater opportunities for funding at the local level. States must persist in seeking alternative funding for the recreation, park, and conservation responsibilities.

Environment

In the late 1960s and the 1970s environment issues that received much attention. Rachel Carson's *Silent Spring* helped awaken a nation to environmental concerns of the environment and ecology. Congress passed a host of legislation dealing with the environment. Some of the legislation dealt with clean air, water pollution, toxic waste, noise abatement and so forth. In the 1980s environmental concerns fell

---

[2]Herbers, John. "For Captives of Federalism, It's Not Going to Get Better Soon." Governing States and Localities. 2 (3) December, 1988, 9.

out of the spotlight they had enjoyed in earlier decades. Problems did not go away, but a national concern about the economy, budget deficits, and trade imbalance gained greater national concern from many. Monies, legislation, and enforcement declined during this period. As the 1980s drew to a close there appeared to be a renewed interest in the environment. The Naisbitt Group (Megatrends) has suggested two trends for the 21st century. The first is a "move from competition to cooperation," and the second is "from complacency to competency." Both of these could improve opportunities for greater environmental concerns" during the 1990s. The Issues Management Association, in 1987, suggested that increased awareness over the next 5 years would be directed toward environmental concerns pertaining to health, safety, and particularly air and water pollution.

The recreation and parks profession has long been a leader in the conservation and environmental movement. That leadership must continue into the nineties. In 1971, William E. Brown, in Islands of Hope, stated, "The recreation and park profession is better informed on environmental matters than the general public--this is our business; it is idealistically motivated to preserve, to fight for the betterment of the environment and the quality of human life..."[3]

Increasing Demand for Recreation

The 1986 report by the President's Commission on American's Outdoors highlights the growing demand for recreation at all levels of government. The report identified 3 major trends directly related to recreation and parks: 1) a slowing of the growth of participation in outdoor recreation; 2) a trend towards more physical active participation; and 3) a growing diversification of outdoor recreation activities in which the public participates.

Marion Clawson wrote that the decline in participant growth cannot be seen as a sign of balance between demand and opportunity. Demand is complicated by increasing interest in activities that are close to home in parks that are already perceived as crowded.[4] The 1986 report suggested that if demand is to be met additional facilities and resources need to be acquired and/or developed. A key proposal was the creation of a permanent, annual $1 billion fund available to all levels of government.

President's Commission on Americans Outdoors

The President's Commission on Americans Outdoors (PCAO) reported a number of findings. Two work groups were particularly important in identifying trends at a national level. One group, representing many different parts of society, addressed strategic planning for outdoor recreation. A series of strategic planning sessions was held between November 1985, and July 1986, in eight different locations throughout the United States. The sessions culminated in a report of 10 trends:
- Changing social and demographic composition. American society is aging, increasing its ethnic mix and its education level, changing its work patterns and creating new centers of population.
- Fluctuating energy availability and cost. Travel and tourism, and recreation activities dependent on energy, will continually be faced by uncertainties based upon day-by-day changes in world market and political conditions.
- Technological innovations. New products and new ways of doing work greatly increase the choices for using leisure time, but can also change demands on recreation providers.
- Shifts in political power closer to the people. State and local governments have shown initiatives in problem solving and assuming responsibilities while the Federal government has been reducing its regulatory and financial assistance roles.

---

[3]Brown, William E., Islands of Hope, National Recreation and Park Association, Arlington, VA, 1971, 194 p.

[4]The President's Commission on American's Outdoors, "Report on Outdoor Recreation Demand: An Overview," Working Papers, Washington, D.C.: U.S. Government Printing Office, 1986.

- Increased accountability of institutions, and leaders, People are participating in public processes to plan programs and formulate policies, and private institutions are being required to make available more information on products and plans.
- Concerns for the environment. Public interest and involvement in environmental protection issues remain high, with more emphasis now being placed on threats to personal environmental health and safety than on threats to nature.
- Creation of innovative partnerships. Cooperative efforts between and among public and private sectors are developing to more efficiently meet public demand for recreation and other services and opportunities.
- Shifts in economic strengths and weaknesses. The evolving global economy and its consequent impacts on a domestic shift from manufacturing to a service and information orientation causes changes in time and money available for recreation.
- Recreation and leisure changes. Development of new equipment, changes in lifestyles, and the variability of the leisure fashion of the moment, place strong pressures on the ability of providers to respond to changing demands.
- Changes in transportation systems. Near completion of the interstate highway system, deregulation of airline and bus travel, and downsizing of the automobile are altering how, when, and where citizens travel for pleasure.[5]

At the conclusion of the strategic planning process a capstone session was held to evaluate all input and to assess trends from sessions as well as the initial session reported above. The 10 trends from this group show some similarities, but have a greater emphasis upon recreation and parks issues.

- Resource protection
- Conflicting uses of recreation lands
- Funding operations and maintenance
- Access (social or physical)
- Roles and relationships
- Benefits of recreation
- Acquisition of open space
- Liability
- Alternate funding sources
- Public education[6]

A National Conference on Recreation and the American City was held in Baltimore, Maryland in May 1986. The conference focused on urban recreation and park concerns and issued six recommendations.

- Perceived differences between urban and nonurban recreation resources and public values should be minimized.
- A more adequate level of capital funding for acquiring, developing, and rehabilitating public recreation resources and facilities is imperative if existing resources are to be protected, future recreation space reserved now, and special natural or cultural sites preserved.
- Increased recognition--political, social and ecological--of recreation values and land and water needs is imperative if recreation resource goals, plans, and protection strategies are to be implemented and sustained.
- Present research and technical communication processes are inadequate. "Clearinghouse" functions--data collection, and dissemination management, technology sharing, opportunity for civic and professional contact, and research--are critical to more efficient public services, resource protection, and general support for recreation and park objectives.
- More effective interagency and intergovernmental cooperation is essential to enhance public and private recreation opportunities and should be pursued at all levels.

---

[5]President's Commission on American's Outdoors, "Summary of Strategic Planning Sessions,:"Working Papers, December, 1986

[6]ibid.

- Civic activists, professional recreation and park managers, planners, and others must be more aware of and responsive to rapid demographic, social, and economic change.[7]

Infrastructure

America's infrastructure, at all levels, is in serious shape. Congresses' Joint Economic Committee reports that the price tax for infrastructure work needed in the next 15 years is around $1 trillion. The National Council on Public Works Improvement, a congressional appointed council, called for a 100% increase in infrastructure capital investment. Part of the problem is that in many cities major public structures were built all at once, and are wearing out at the same time. Local and state agencies are not alone in suffering from infrastructure problems. A Government Accounting Office report suggested the National Park Service would experience $1.9 billion in maintenance shortfall. In a 1987 study sponsored by the International City Managers Association, 43% of the respondents indicated their recreation and park infrastructure was in need of repair or, that they planned expansion in the near future.[8]

The way these issues are addressed in the 1990s will have an impact on recreation and park funding at all levels. Lance Simmons, the Conference of Mayors' assistant executive director for legislative affairs said, "In the past 8 years we have seen a significant shift back to local governments that don't have adequate resources to do everything. When it comes to choices between human capital and physical capital, the most compassionate, most reasonable avenue is toward human capital, not to say that physical capital and federal investment are not crucial and important, but human capital comes first.:[9] The President's Commission on Americans Outdoors recommended that local, state, and federal officials plan and budget for systematic renovation and replacement of existing facilities.

Social Structure Problems

AIDS, the homeless, the graying of the American population are issues that have changed the nature of the family considerably over the past 10 years. The traditional nuclear family is rapidly giving way to the single parent family. In many urban areas the single parent family outnumbers the traditional nuclear family. This is especially the case among those who receive welfare. As more and more women enter the work force, the need for quality daycare increases. During the 1990s, recreation and park professionals must address these issues and other social problems. A 1976 Canadian study suggested that by 1995, recreation departments would be renamed departments of human services. This is already happening in some communities in the United States. As recreation and park professionals adjust to meet these changing social conditions they will need to rethink the way departments are run, and the types of services they provide. Some issues of concern are:
- The way services are to be provided to a graying population.
- The most effective delivery patterns for meeting the diverse social needs of communities.
- The types of efforts that are being made to meet the needs of special populations.
- The way the changing family is addressed in programs and services.
- The way values that support wise use of leisure are being assessed or applied in the provision of services and facilities to a changing population.

---

[7]President's Commission on American's Outdoors, "National Conference on Recreation and the American City," Working Papers, December, 1986

[8]International City Managers Association, 1988 - The Municipal Yearbook, Washington, D.C., 459 p.

[9]"American City and County Survey on Infrastructure Needs," American City and County, November, 1988, 33-36.

Funding Issues for the Future

Land and Water Conservation Fund

The Land and Water Conservation Fund (LWCF), an outgrowth of the Outdoor Recreation Resources Review Commission report, was initiated in 1964 under the Johnson administration. It is a trust fund drawing from revenues from the sale of oil leases from the outer continental shelf. As of 1988, the fund contained almost $6 billion.

The LWCF has been a captive of political process since its inception. During the 1960s and early 1970s when funding was high (sometimes higher than anticipated), there was little complaint about the program. All levels of government benefited from the fund. Beginning with the Carter administration and continuing into the Reagan administration, the fund fell on hard times. Inflation and deficit reduction were reasons forwarded for proposing low or no funding. Congress has maintained funding at a low level.

Whereas the fund initially benefited all levels of government, in recent years the bulk of the funding has gone to federal recreation and park agencies for land acquisition. For example, in 1989, $202 million was appropriated, of which only $20 million was available to the 50 states to share. Funding has been reduced 91% since a 1977 high of $175 million was made available to the states.

The call has been, and will continue to be, to establish a trust from which LWCF monies would be drawn. Establishment of a trust would conceivably take the appropriation process away from congress and insure a consistent level of funding available to various levels of government.
On the negative side, opponents to such legislation suggest that the $6 billion dollar reserve does not really exist. The money has been spent and the fund exists merely as an accounting code. To establish a fund with no congressional oversight would 1) increase the already record deficit, and 2) would not address the issue of maintenance of existing lands, but only acquisition of new federal lands. Regardless of what type of legislation affecting the LWCF is forthcoming during the 1990s, it is almost certain that some legislation will be enacted. Its impact upon recreation and parks could be significant.

State and Local Sources of Funds

In the 1980s, state and local level governments had to be more innovative than at any time in history in order to meet the needs of recreation and park systems. Governments have sought new ways to raise revenues. State and local agencies have made marketing an essential element of the revenue plan. States and some local governments market heavily for the tourist trade in an effort to increase state revenue.

Competition/Cooperation with the Private Sector

At the heart of this issue is the question of who has responsibility for what. Traditional patterns for provision of recreation and park services changed following the taxpayer revolt of the late 1970s and early 1980s. Some communities went partially or entirely to private industry to provide recreation services and maintenance of facilities. Former Secretary of the Interior, Donald Hodel, called for the elimination of 2000 positions within the Department of the Interior and their replacement with private contractors.

A recent study of municipalities reported that 18% of the respondents currently contracted out for recreation and park services, either wholly or partially, and that 10% contracted their facilities to private management. The study also reported that 21% plan to contract services and 12% to contract facilities to private management in the next two years.[10]

The traditional role of recreation has been confused as the private sector has moved into recreation and fitness. Competition between the private and public sector has been good and bad. In some cases

---

[10]International City Managers Association, 1988 - The Municipal Yearbook, Washington, D.C., 459 p.

competition has given way to cooperation. PCAO recommended that communities develop strong, public-private partnerships with neighborhood and non-profit groups to improve recreation services, committing more time, money and patience to cooperative ventures among public agencies and between the public and private sectors.

Roles

Recent political and economic changes and future trends will shape recreation and parks. Institutional changes will determine how the roles of recreation and parks are perceived in society. Recreation and park professional, board members, and concerned citizens must fit into a changing pattern. The future of recreation and parks in the government sector must be determined Professionals must define roles for themselves as they shape their own futures.

The decentralization of the public policy making process means that more and more decisions are being made at state and local levels. Recreation and park professionals and board members have a greater chance of making their voices heard than ever before.

To influence decisions, learn the players and the rules in the political game.

- Find out who is responsible for making a decision.
- Discover what processes they intend to use to make the decisions.
- Learn which mechanisms are available for public input.
- Find out what sort of time line the decision makers are working under.
- Discover who else needs to give approval.
- Find out when will the decision will go into effect.

Because each state is different, there is no single blueprint for action. The problems of each state must be addressed individually. Persistence, curiosity and commitment are important. Continue to question the way decisions are made and the way government works. Be curious about what motivates decision makers. A belief that recreation and parks can and must be a part of the national agenda for the future can maintain momentum through disappointments faced on the way to winning an important game.

3

Know the State Legislature

Diverse levels of recreation and park agencies within a state often make decision making a fragmentary process. The state recreation and parks director has the opportunity to make some decisions that affect local recreation and park agencies, county agencies, and most specifically, the state agency. State legislatures, which authorize appropriations, create or modify law, and access taxes, affect recreation and park agencies at all levels. State legislatures may choose to give up any portion of their primary authority for making decisions to the state recreation and park agency, county, or municipal agencies.

A Public Forum

The United States system of government is based largely on a conflict resolution model. Because ours is a representative democracy which allows every adult a voice, many diverse opinions, attitudes, and values are played out. Opinions vary about the latitude and power government should exercise in public problems. While conflicts are sometimes resolved in the courts, more often they are resolved in the legislatures which provide a mechanism for the open debate of public issues. Legislatures are a forum in which conflict can be resolved and compromises made in a protected and regulated environment. Safe and open forums for public controversy, legislatures make the business of government, the business of the people open to public scrutiny. Many observers believe that providing a safe, appropriate, and constructive mechanism for conflict resolution has helped ensure the longevity of our system of government.

The federal government and its legislative branch, the United States Congress, is concerned with global issues, such as foreign policy, defense, and interstate commerce, as well as domestic policy. By contrast, state legislatures devote themselves primarily to internal domestic policy. Understandably, the United States Congress is more complex and institutionalized in its structure and functions than are state legislatures. The federal government requires a full time Congress and full time support staff. Because state legislatures meet less frequently, state legislators are usually part-time and have other careers and limited staff.

Characteristics of State Legislatures

State legislatures are as different as they are alike. Each state has unique laws, procedures, values, and traditions which undergird its legislature. There are some similarities, and when viewed together, state legislatures take on some general characteristics which can prove useful. Keep in mind that all characteristics may not apply to each state in each instance (Figure 3.1 shows specific information for each state).

All states except Nebraska have bicameral legislatures. Bicameral legislatures are modeled on the English parliamentary system of government, and consist of two houses, an upper house called the senate, and a lower house called the house of representatives. In some states, the state legislature is called the general assembly or legislative assembly. Senators usually serve 4 years and representatives usually serve for 2 years.

Legislators, like Congressmen, are elected from geographic political districts. In the early days of our country, state political districts were nothing more than communities or neighborhoods. Population numbers were not a consideration. Today, stringent laws and guidelines define political boundaries. Regular provisions for redistricting ensure the "one man, one vote" concept and prevent illegal gerrymandering.

Population generally governs the geographic boundaries of a political district. Most states have single member districts in which one members is elected from each district. Some states have multimember districts which elect more than one legislator per district.

State legislatures have traditionally met biennially, or once every 2 years, although the recent trend is to meet annually. More legislatures are meeting in off years in either regular, budgetary, special, or work sessions than they have in the past. Forty-three states now meet annually. So-called special sessions may be convened either by the legislature or the governor, depending on the state constitution and statutes. Most special sessions must be called to deal with a specific topic. Discussion of other items during this time is prohibited.

Other trends apparent in state legislatures include the development and expansion of professional staff, the reform of legislative rules and procedures, the expansion of legislative budget review capacity, and the development of statutes on ethics, campaign finance, disclosure, and conflict of interest.

Most states limit the length of their legislative sessions by statute or constitution. The typical state legislature meets from January through May or June. Some meet into the summer, or hold frequent special sessions. Less than six meet year round. The state legislative season, which is usually in winter, is an agrarian society holdover. Early farmer-legislators came to the capitol after the harvest and Christmas holidays and concluded business in time to return home for spring planting.

Legislative Leadership

In all states except Nebraska, the presiding officer in the lower house is the speaker of the house, chosen by and from the majority party on a vote of the whole house. In the senate, the presiding officer is the president or president pro tem. Some states designate the lieutenant governor as the official president of the senate, and where this occurs, the majority party elects a president pro tem to serve in his absence.

As in the United States Congress, decisions are made through a committee structure in state legislatures. All legislatures have a statutory set of standing committees which deal with special problems or categories of issues. Legislators usually serve on three or more committees. Typical of the 10-30 standing committees in each house are agriculture, education, energy and natural resources, commerce, health and welfare, local government, government operations, transportation, rules, labor, judiciary, housing, appropriations and finance. The importance of a particular topic to the state determines whether or not it is designated as a standing committee. Some states may combine agriculture and natural resource, or education, health and welfare, while others have separate standing committees for each of these areas. Rules committees generally determine procedural rules for the senate and house. In some states they have the power to determine the way and in what manner a bill is considered, and who may speak to it on the floor.

The primary shaping of legislation occurs in committees, on the floor. Legislatures have also become more active between sessions in the interim period. Often, this is the time when more in-depth studies are carried out and legislation is drafted by support staff.

Appropriations committees designate how much money will go to a particular program, usually biennially. Some states also have budget committees and/or finance committees which may set limits on total appropriations, evaluate income sources (taxation and revenue), or concern themselves more with the state's financial well-being than with specific program appropriations.

Most states have committees that include recreation and park issues as part of their concerns. The committees have a variety of names, such as the natural resources committee. Other committees that receive recreation and park issues are ways and means, local government, agriculture, and energy.

During the course of a biennium, a state legislature, like Congress, may introduce a large number of bills, but may pass very few of them. During the 1984-1985 legislative session, for example, almost 200,000 bills were introduced nation wide. Utah, Vermont, and Wyoming each had less than 1,000 bills introduced while New York had in excess of 3,300 bills introduced. Ohio enacted less than 200 bills and California enacted over 3,000 bills. Twenty-five states allow bills introduced in the first year of a biennium to be carried into the second year. This amounts to an average of 50,000 bills.

Characteristics of State Legislators

Just as each state is different, so too is every state legislator. A composite portrait can be a useful frame of reference by which to know a legislator better. The state constitution lists minimum qualifications for state legislators, relative to age, citizenship, and residence. By occupation, lawyers, businessmen, full time legislators,and agricultural occupations are the most common reported in state legislatures. Women comprise only a little more than 15% of the legislators. Although there are more men than women legislators, women are more heavily represented in the western states and New England. Many legislators were either born in, or have lived for many years in their legislative districts. More than three-fourth of them have had some college education, and they tend to mirror the major religious preference of the district they represent.

Currently there are 7,461 state legislators nationwide -- 5,466 in the house, and 1,995 in the senate. The average state has 40 state senators and 109 representatives in the house. New Hampshire has the largest number of representatives with 400 house members, and Minnesota has the largest number of senators with 67. Alaska ranks the lowest with 40 senators and 40 representatives.

Fifty-nine percent of all state senators belong to the Democratic party. Thirty-eight percent belong to the Republican party. Three percent belong to other parties. In the house, 60% of the members are Democrats, and 40% are Republican. Some states, such as Alabama, Arkansas, and Mississippi, which virtually have a one party system, often play out conflicts within party factions instead of between two parties.[11]

Legislator--A Moonlight Career

Unlike congressmen, state legislators tend to view their work as a part-time job, as the legislature is in session only part of the year. Most state legislatures have staff lawyers to assist with the technical work of drafting bills, as well as some form of legislative reference service. California legislators enjoy complete office facilities and staffs, including lawyers and secretaries, while some states offer neither offices nor permanent staffs, preferring to hire temporary employees and house legislators in hotels when the legislature is in session.

Compared with Congress, state legislatures have met less, been paid less, concerned themselves with a much narrower agenda, maintained smaller staffs, and maintained more modest office space (or none at all) for their members. While this is still true today, the complexities of state government, the new emphasis on federalism, and the need to act as competent and efficient receivers of federal funds have pressured state governments to diversify and grow. The trend in state legislatures is to increase staff, office space, salaries, length of legislative session, and number of special and working sessions. In some very real ways, the job of governing domestic programs is increasingly shifting to the states.

---

[11]The Council of State Governments, The Book of the States, 1989-90. Volume 27, Lexington, KY, 523 p.

Salaries

Salaries for legislators have grown in recent years in some states, although the salary range among states is very great. Of the 38 states which pay their legislator on an annual basis the average salary for a state legislator is $18,758.

Five states compensated their legislators more than $40,000 per year. New York pays the highest at $43,000, A few states pay their legislators for each day the legislature is in session, or by some system other than an annual salary. Additionally, legislators, in all but six states, receive per diem and/or are compensated for travel, office expenses, retirement, and medical benefits. These benefits vary widely.

The salary range among state legislators is wide, and their tasks and duties vary enormously as well. Illogical enough, however, there is probably not a direct correlation nationwide between number of legislative days worked and salary. Forty-one states have removed salaries from constitutional restrictions. In nine states salaries are still set in the constitution.

State legislatures are also characterized by high turnover, higher at the state than at the federal level. The average turnover rate in state senates in 1986-87 was 20%, the average turnover rate in the house was 23%. The high turnover rate has been attributed, among other things, to low pay, the part-time nature of the job, and the length of time between biennial meetings. Some observers feel that some state legislators serve their term and then return to their own professions. Legislators who are motivated use the state legislature as a stepping stone, and move on to follow higher political aspirations.

One observer of state legislators studied the recruitment of freshmen legislators in Connecticut, and later interviewed them. On the basis of this data, he was able to group them into four broad categories: as spectators, who watch what goes on; as advertisers, who participate for public relations purposes; as reluctants, who have been drafted by the party; and as lawmakers, who are interested in mastering the legislative process and passing legislation. A legislator may fit into any one or none of these categories. To be effective in influencing public policy, know what forces move the legislator who handles each important issue.

How a Bill Becomes a Law

Passing legislation on the state level is similar to federal law process. Although each state has individual idiosyncrasies, the basic elements are similar. There are at least nine general steps common to most states (Figure 3.1).

Introduction

Although all bills must be introduced by a legislator, the idea for a bill can come from anyone. In a state with a strong executive, the governor can frame a piece of legislation. On the state level, as on the national level, special interest groups often draw up bills they they want their legislators to introduce. In states which have comparatively small staffs, this reduces the burden on the legislator and ensures that the interest group gets exactly what it wants, at least at the beginning of the legislative process.

How well a bill does in the legislature often depends on its sponsors. In general, the more prestigious the sponsor, the more likelihood passage is. Sometimes a bill is cosponsored by two or more representatives. Bills may be introduced in either house.

First Reading

Each bill is given three readings, a tradition historically based in the philosophy of open government. Originally, each bill was given three readings so that all legislators (even those who could not read) would know the contents of the bill, keeping the public's business public. It also allowed ample time for

Figure 3.3 How a Bill Becomes a Law

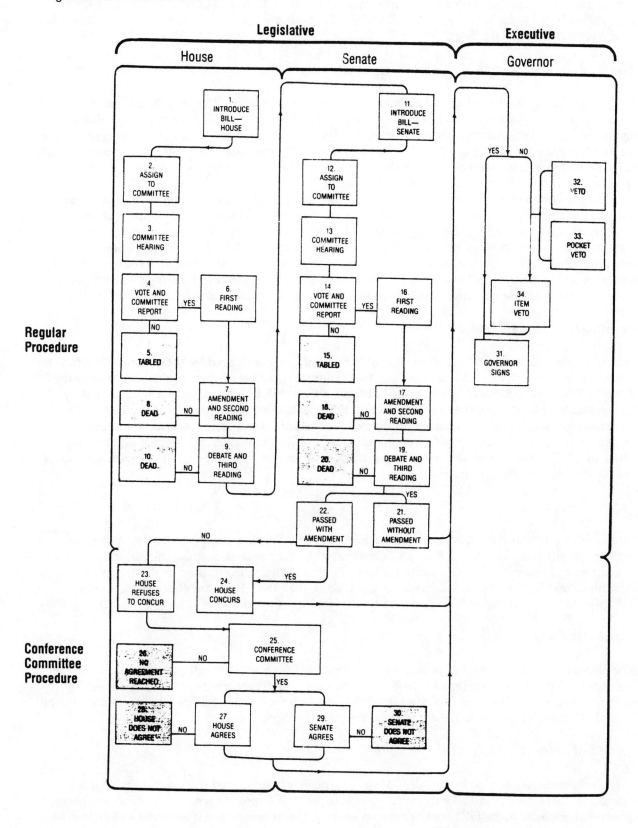

legislators to prepare their arguments before considering the bill in committee. Today, bills are not always "read" out loud, but may be considered on three different occasions, or the title may be read--a hold over from the old readings.

The Bill is Placed in Committee

After the bill has been introduced, it is printed and referred to a committee by the speaker of the house or the president of the senate. In Congress, most of the real work on a bill, debate, introduction of amendments, and negotiating, goes on in the committees. In the states, however, more attention is given to floor work, as committees are less structured. Whereas the congressional committee chair is usually responsible for guiding the bill through the committee and onto the floor, in the states, the bill's sponsor or patron monitors and pushes the bill through.

Because state legislatures are in session part-time, and because they focus on floor action rather than committees, the power of political parties is strengthened. The relative smallness of their districts encourages state legislators to be parochial in their interests. They may often barter for votes on legislation which benefits their district, and pledge their votes on a bill that is irrelevant to their constituents. This vote-trading is often done in party legislative caucuses. Unlike most committee meetings which are open to the public, party caucuses limit the openness of the legislative process. They also demonstrate how important constituent input is in legislative decision making.

Committee Consideration

The committee chair determines when the bill is called up, or considered by the committee--which for some bills is never. When a bill is called up, the committee may hear public testimony for or against the bill. The committee may approve the bill as is, kill the bill by voting against it, change it by offering amendments, refer the bill to a subcommittee, or take no action, which also kills the bill.

If the bill is approved, it is placed on the house calendar. Some states may have specific procedures set down by the Rules Committee for placing bills on the calendar, and for determining when, and how to structure debate. In states with less stringent requirements, the legislative leaders usually decide the rules for debate.

Second Reading

On the bill's calendar date, the bill has its second reading. This is an important step. With this reading the bill is brought to the floor and debated by the entire house membership which may offer amendments or may kill the bill. Debate may be limited by the rule attached to the bill by the Rules Committee and by the way the leaders choose to enforce the rules. This can often depend on how they feel about the bill. Voting on the second reading is often by voice vote.

Third Reading

After the second reading, the bill is engrossed, or reprinted with amendments, and it appears on the calendar for a third reading. Debate is often waived, and new amendments are usually passed by unanimous consent. Then the final vote is taken, usually by roll call. If defeated at this stage, the bill is dead. If passed, it is sent to the other house for consideration.

Second House Consideration

State consideration of the bill by the second house is much less structured than in Congress. If it is referred to committee, it will take the same path as in the first house. In some states if no one presents substantial opposition, the bill may not even be referred to committee, but go straight to the floor for debate and amendment. If the bill passes in both houses in the same form, it goes to the governor for signature.

Conference Committee

If the bill passes with amendments which make it different from the version passed in the first house, then the bill goes to a joint conference committee. The conference committee is comprised of members from each house who try to work out a compromise agreeable to both houses. If agreement cannot be reached, the bill cannot pass. If compromise is reached, the compromise version is returned to both houses for final vote. If both houses pass the revised conference committee version, the bill passes the legislature and goes to the governor for signature.

The Governor's Veto Power

A bill is not officially a law until it is signed by the governor. In all states except North Carolina, the governor has the power to veto a bill passed by the state legislature. Although states have provided for their legislatures to override the governor's veto, the problems inherent in reassembling part-time legislatures, and compiling enough votes to override make the governor's veto powerful. The governors, like the President, can also use a *pocket veto*, which means that the bill dies because the governor simply does not sign it. Unlike a regular veto, the governor does not have to take a specific negative action to kill the bill in a pocket veto, but can simply take no action.

Unlike the President, some governors have a third option called an *item veto*. An item veto means that the governor can veto a particular item, usually in an appropriations bill, without vetoing the entire bill. Item vetos are an attempt by the governors to control the influence of special interest groups on the legislature.

Registration of Lobbyists

Although the First Amendment to the Constitution guarantees "the right of the people . . . to petition the government for a redress of grievances," Congress and the states place some restrictions on lobbying activities and require disclosure of certain information. Associations considering this type of activity need to be aware of legal ramifications. Before lobbying directly, contact the state lobbying registration office for specific information.

Federal requirements relating to lobbying activities fall under income tax laws and lobbying registration laws. Compliance with income tax laws attracts most concern as failure to comply can be costly. The IRS code categorizes individual membership organizations, and the like. Most state associations fall under section 501(c) (3)--Religious, charitable, scientific, literary, educational, testing for public safety, fostering national or international amateur sports competition, and prevention of cruelty to children and animals organizations.

Most membership associations with goals of professional development and continuing education fall within the education category. Education, in this case refers to "instruction of the individual and the community." Although this definition comes close to popular understandings of lobbying, advocacy of a particular position is generally allowed as long as a "full and fair exposition of the pertinent facts" is presented.

Organizations which "contact, or urge the public to contact members of a legislative body for purposes of proposing, supporting, or opposing legislation--or advocate the adoption or rejection of legislation" are said to engage in legislative activity. There also exists an apparent distinction between activities designed to "persuade" and activities designed to "educate" with only the former being considered lobbying activity.

The IRS 501(c) (3) rules state that "no substantial part" of these organizations' activities may consist of "carrying propaganda or otherwise attempting to influence legislation." "Substantial part" has been variously defined by IRS audit guidelines and case law as anything from 5% to 20%.

States

In addition to federal IRS laws, states have additional requirements for lobbyists. In general, public education and professional opinion or testimony is not considered to be lobbying but each state's laws should be checked if substantial lobbying activities are planned. Often, lobbying requires only annual registration and quarterly financial disclosure statements to ensure that lobbying is not one of the organization's principle activities. Registration, then, may well be an appropriate move for an association.

Every state has different laws regarding registration, but 33 states make an exception for persons who speak only before committees or boards. Thirty-nine make exceptions for public officials acting in an official capacity; 16 make exception for any persons with professional knowledge acting as a professional witness. These exceptions could constitute all the lobbying an organization plans to do.
In terms of defining who is a lobbyist on the state level the following definitions are the most common:
- 43 states: Anyone who receives compensation to influence legislative action.
- 23 states: Anyone who spends money to influence legislation.
- 19 states: Anyone who represents someone else's interests.
- 7 states: Any executive branch employee who attempts to influence legislation.

(Note: Source--Council of State Governments, *Book of States, 1988-89*)
To register as a lobbyist, contact the secretary of state, clerk of the house, ethics commission or state legislative council. State procedures, like definitions vary.

Members of an association who plan a large, substantial legislative campaign or lobbying effort, have another alternative. They can form a separate organization specifically for lobbying purposes, a "friends of" organization. While this may not be legally necessary, an organization may prefer to clearly distinguish between strictly professional and advocacy activities. Such a move could also broaden a political base by including parents and other supporters.

4

Planning Legislative Action

Playing the political game

Planning legislative action is much like planning anything else. To be effective:

- Establish a clear goal.
- Decide the steps to be taken to accomplish the goal.
- Make an action plan with deadlines.
- Evaluate resources.
- Act

Playing the political game is like playing any other game. To play, know the rules. The rules of the legislative game are laws, regulations, and traditions that govern the election of legislators and passage of legislation.

After learning the rules, develop a basic game plan. On offense or defense, sprint at the start, or save energy for a strong finish. Each plan will differ with each new legislative game. Each team is different. Teams develop new skills as they play, and more sophisticated game plans emerge with each encounter.

Along with the game plan, develop a repertoire of plays as the game unfolds. If players are to work together as a team, they all need to know the same plays and signal calls to avoid confusion and embarrassment, or worse, a big loss. Planning ensures that everyone knows the plays needed to win the big game.

Just as in a game, timing is important. No matter how much time is needed to study an issue or to write testimony, the clock keeps ticking. An opponent may call time-out by tabling the bill in committee when the time has come to take action.

There's no way to be absolutely ready for every move an opponent makes, but more practice and preparation will mean a better the chance for success. Knowledge, a feel for the subtleties of the game, and ultimately, expertise will improve with practice.

Remember to give opponents their due. Complete preparation does not absolutely guarantee success. Obviously, there are no guarantees. Watching the strategies of worthy opponents and being part of the legislative process at work can be exciting, and can be preparation for the next game.

Where Do Citizens Stand?

Each state and locality has different issues and problems. As more political decisions about recreation and parks are made at the state and local level, the diversity of issues increases. No one can provide a blueprint for action guaranteed to work in every situation. Because recreation and parks issues are as diverse as the states which house them, legislative problems must be examined individually, within the context of each state's political realities.

Citizens who want to influence public policy must follow a plan designed to support the quirks and intricacies of any state or local government. Learn to approach any problem, in an organized and methodical way, choosing strategies and tactics that will work best. Plan and make a blueprint.

Organization

Organization is the key to any good game. Although a plan can be organized in may different ways, here is one model (Figure 4.1) that has worked well for others. This model sets up a central Legislative Action Committee to coordinate the components of a legislative campaign. The Committee plans, organizes, communicates, and gives direction to the people involved.

The five components of a comprehensive legislative action plan are:

- research
- lobby
- public relations
- grass roots network
- finance and resources.

Not every legislative action will require all five components, but a state-wide, comprehensive plan needs to consider these functions to be thorough and effective.The Legislative Action Committee

The Legislative Action Committee

The function of the Legislative Action Committee is to manage the legislative lobbying campaign. The committee plans legislative action strategies, organizes resources into a functioning and effective lobbying force, coordinates and directs the action of the players, and facilities communication among all participants. The committee can include the association president, public and legislative committee chair, and the state public communications coordinator, or others as desired. Be careful not to make the committee so large that it inhibits decision making. Timely action is the key to legislative success.

Research

The Research Task Force is responsible for providing information for use by other task forces by formulating arguments, providing data to support the legislative initiative, monitoring the opposition's speeches and press clippings, and researching potential supporters. The research task force might write a backgrounder that the Public Relations Task Force could use with the media. It might research the local American Medical Association to determine their philosophical biases, and then write a support statement about the legislation which the lobbyist could take to the AMA for approval. Any support statement has a better chance of being signed and approved if it is already written and if it is consistent with the established philosophy of the anticipated support group. The task force might also prepare charts and graphs for the lobbyist to take to a public hearing. The Research Task Force is comprised of behind the scenes people who provide the ammunition for other task forces.

Lobby

The Lobby Task Force monitors proposed legislation's progress through the House and Senate, organizes specific lobbying activities, and actually lobbies members of the legislature. Members are few, but within easy access to the capitol. They keep track of who is voting for and against the bill, the head count; know where the bill is in the process, legislative tracking; monitor the opposition's progress and arguments; and monitor the legislative leadership's position. The Lobby Task Force is responsible for feeding timely and accurate information to the rest of the committee to assure that the total efforts are coordinated, strategically placed and timed. The task force knows when hearings are being held and chooses the most appropriate people and positions to present testimony.

The task force needs to work closely with the Grass Roots Network so they can appropriately speak to their legislators with the right message. Spending their time on the phone and at the capitol, they know whose support is wavering, and who can be swayed. Task force members need to be committed, hard working, dependable, and within close proximity to the capitol. Without good legislative intelligence, the efforts of the whole group can be misdirected.

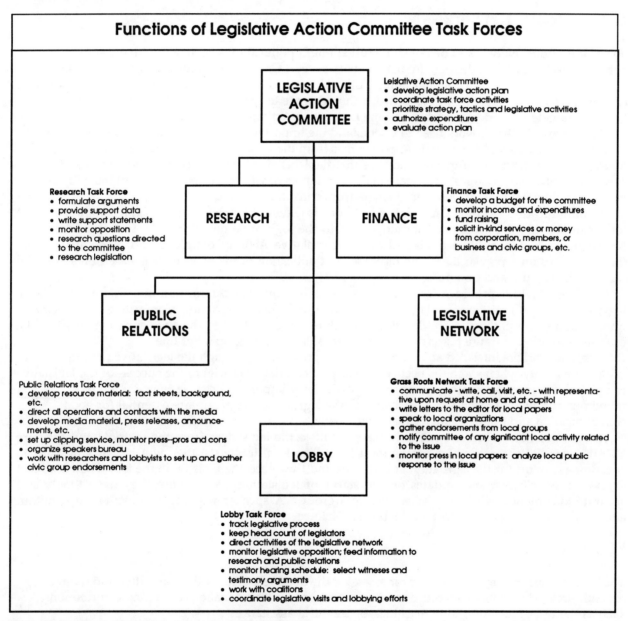

Functions of Legislative Action Committee Task Forces

LEGISLATIVE ACTION COMMITTEE

Leislative Action Committee
- develop legislative action plan
- coordinate task force activities
- prioritize strategy, tactics and legislative activities
- authorize expenditures
- evaluate action plan

RESEARCH

Research Task Force
- formulate arguments
- provide support data
- write support statements
- monitor opposition
- research questions directed to the committee
- research legislation

FINANCE

Finance Task Force
- develop a budget for the committee
- monitor income and expenditures
- fund raising
- solicit in-kind services or money from corporation, members, or business and civic groups, etc.

PUBLIC RELATIONS

Public Relations Task Force
- develop resource material: fact sheets, background, etc.
- direct all operations and contacts with the media
- develop media material, press releases, announcements, etc.
- set up clipping service, monitor press--pros and cons
- organize speakers bureau
- work with researchers and lobbyists to set up and gather civic group endorsements

LEGISLATIVE NETWORK

Grass Roots Network Task Force
- communicate - write, call, visit, etc. - with representative upon request at home and at capitol
- write letters to the editor for local papers
- speak to local organizations
- gather endorsements from local groups
- notify committee of any significant local activity related to the issue
- monitor press in local papers: analyze local public response to the issue

LOBBY

Lobby Task Force
- track legislative process
- keep head count of legislators
- direct activities of the legislative network
- monitor legislative opposition; feed information to research and public relations
- monitor hearing schedule: select witnesses and testimony arguments
- work with coalitions
- coordinate legislative visits and lobbying efforts

Figure 4.1 Functions of Legislative Action Committee Task forces

Public Relations

The Public Relations Task Force directs all media activities for the legislative effort, and serves as the primary conduit to the media. It generates information for the media, prepares press releases, arranges television coverage, solicits radio time, recommends feature articles and prepares fact sheets. This task force also monitors good and bad press, and keeps in close contact with the head of the Lobby Task Force. Members can notify the Grass Roots Network that letters to the editor are needed in a particular area to counterbalance a newspaper's negative editorial stance. They can let the lobbyists know that press about the issue is positive in a legislative opponent's district. Sending press clippings can be very convincing. They can prepare endorsement statements based on intelligence from researchers. Their main task is to take information from the Research Task Force, and interpret it to the public simply, clearly, and intelligibly. They can also help the lobbyists prepare clean and easy to understand testimony and fact sheets for distribution at hearings and press luncheons.

Grass Roots Network

For a Grass Roots Network to demonstrate full-strength political muscle, it should have at least one person in each legislative district. In districts with several Grass Roots Networks, one person should serve as the contact person, communicating to others by post card or by telephone network. Upon request, each individual participating in the network should write telegrams, and call or visit a legislator who has been targeted as a decision maker by the Legislative Action Committee.

Participants in the network need to understand the importance of their function. As constituents, they demonstrate to legislators that support comes from their own districts, not just from state capitol lobbyists. Networkers reinforce the message that the legislator has received from lobbyists and the press, and notes the messages' pertinence to the legislator's constituency. No amount of lobbying at the capitol can do what several well placed letters from constituents can do.

Communicating with the Grass Roots Network is essential for the success of the committee. Two tools can provide the necessary communication to the legislative network. The first is a Legislative Newsletter, which should be published by the Legislative Action Committee and made available to the task forces on a regular basis (see figure #.#). Publication of the newsletter is based on actions by the state legislature and Congress.

The second tool provides for quick responses to time-dated information. If, for example, a legislative sub-committee reports a bill out that the Legislative Action Committee and needs an immediate response, the use of a legislative hot-line can be critical to the success of the efforts. The example provided in figure #.# is one method available for setting up a hot-line.

Keep networkers informed about how the bill is progressing through the legislative process. Don't call on them only when a letter is needed. Their participation is crucial to the success of the legislative campaign. Active participating networkers--particularly important because they are the most numerous and widely dispersed participants in the legislative campaign--are essential for good communication and timing. Plan for their involvement.

Legislative networkers are not only the conduit to the legislators from the districts, but they are also the voice of the committee on the local level. As local lobbyists, they will be working hard to encourage support for the legislation in their area and they need the tools to do the job. They need fact sheets, press releases, and updates on the status of legislation. Make sure they have timely and accurate information when they speak before a group. A speaker without documentation is not an effective spokes person. Support local lobbyists.Finance

Finance

The Finance Task Force is responsible for assessing the fiscal resources of the committee and monitoring expenditures. The finance committee can also raise money, solicit donations or in kind contributions, such as the use of facilities, copy machines, or technical assistance.

Planning

The first task of the Legislative Action Committee is to plan. Establish a game plan and start the players in motion. Planning means making decisions about what must be done in a methodical way.

Good planning keeps projects on track, assures unity of purpose, and helps the group to focus in times of crisis. Plan work, and work the plan. Planning for legislative action is the same as planning for anything else. Good planning means answering the who, what, why, when and how questions.

What

Name the goal to be accomplished. Make the goal a positive statement.

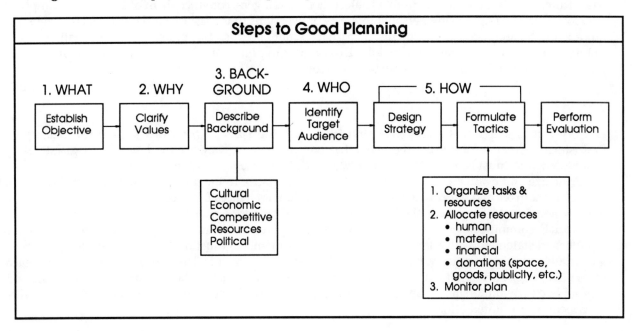

Figure 4.2 Steps to Good Planning

Why

Explain why the problem deserves the attention and resources set to be put behind it. Describe why the organization's values and priorities require this involvement. State reasons positively.

Background

Examine the problem more closely. Describe the way the issue come about. Name the political, economic, and cultural forces that affect it. Background on the issue will help put the problem in a larger context and define it more clearly. Background information helps in understanding the problem, so that a solution can be planned.

Who

Identify a target audience. Identify the people who must be influenced. Persuade and lobby those people.Find out who has jurisdiction over an issue. It may be the state legislative branch or the executive branch. The favored bill may be stuck in a Senate subcommittee. The local school board or the board of supervisors may make the final decision in a local issue. Find out who, if anyone, has overt, indirect, or covert power in the matter. Seek a friend in power, someone to whom there is ready access. Know who will be the easiest to influence, as well as the most difficult. Be able to name the decision makers and the people to whom they listen.

How

Evaluate the game plan. Use strategies that will reach a target audience. Be prepared to provide basic education about an issue. Be able to alert them to dangers, convince them of benefits, or simply overcome biases. Explore any personal interests or aversions to the issue. Find out if legislators listen more to big business, their constituents, or perhaps school boards. Use systems that are available for public input. Reach legislators informally Explore useful public relations tactics. Use personal or professional contacts. All members can be resources.

Tactics

Identify tactics which will accomplish strategies. Use the *Tools for the Media* section for ideas. Brainstorm. Create. Tactics are the plays that win the game. They are the heart of a legislative action plan, and must be well chosen, organized, deadline oriented and tight.

Prioritize and evaluate tactics in terms of their importance to the intended outcome, the human and financial resources and effort which they require, and their chances for success. (Once again: who, what, when, how!) Each tactic the Legislative Action Committee chooses is assigned to an appropriate committee member, or task force chair and given a timeline. Assign a member to respond to a published statement with a letter to an editor. Other members must be provided with the postage for a legislative mailing. Someone else must write a support statement. These efforts must reinforce each other. The Legislative Action Committee formulates a plan that sets wheels in motion. A solid, thorough, clearly understood plan allows many people across the state to work on a common goal with an effective and united effort.

1. WHAT:

OBJECTIVE: To identify the desired outcome. What do you want to accomplish?

2. WHY:

VALUES: Why should we address this issue?

3. Back-Ground:

Identify variables that have an impact on the objective:
- cultural/social
- economic
- competition
- resources
- political/legal

4. WHO:

TARGET AUDIENCE: Who do we want to influence?

5. HOW:

STRATEGY: What strategies can we use to reach our target groups and accomplish our goals?

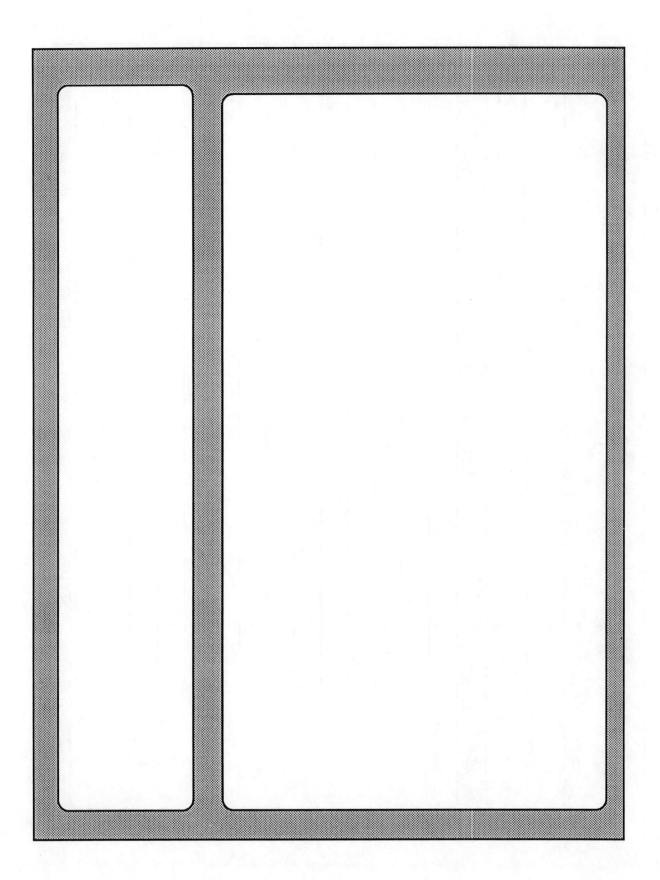

name

association

For Strategy No.

Objective:

Target Audience

• Level

• Branch

Strategies:

Target Audience _____

Strategy _____

page _____

Tactics:

Personnel	Resources	Miscellaneous

WHAT _____

WHEN _____

WHERE _____

WHAT _____

WHEN _____

WHERE _____

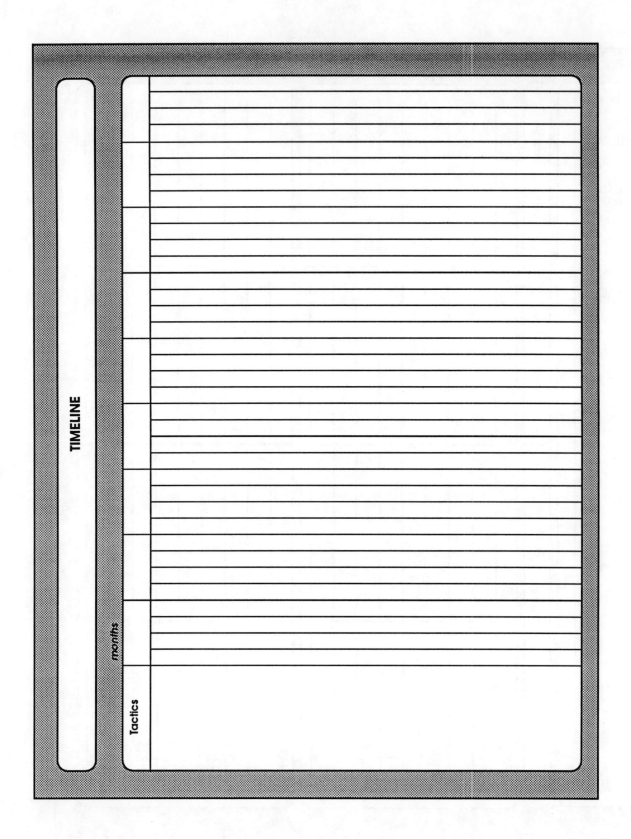

TIMELINE

months

Tactics

1. WHAT:

OBJECTIVE: To identify the desired outcome. What do you want to accomplish?

The objective of this legislative action plan is to create a state Council on Recreation and Parks.

2. WHY:

VALUES: Why should we address this issue?

We believe that two divergent tracks in recreation and parks have developed in Central State. The resource track has been well funded and supported by the state. The human services track needs to receive similar attention by the state. The development of a Council on Recreation and Parks will tie the two tracks together, create improved communication, and expand Central states economic future.

3. Back-Ground:

Identify variables that have an impact on the objective:
- cultural/social
- economic
- competition
- resources
- political/legal

The two tracks to the provision of recreation and parks have existed simultaneously within most states and in many ways are compatible, but in other ways are not. Resource-oriented management concentrates its efforts on outdoor recreation resources in an acceptance of the land ethic. It changes the role of man from the conqueror of the land community to a member and citizen of it. To this end, agencies involved in the provision of these resources concentrate on the acquisition, preservation, development and construction of recreation facilities and resources. Individuals using these resources are expected to provide their own recreation activity; the resource serving as a locational opportunity for that activity to occur on.

In contrast, municipal, private non-profit, and some county agencies provide human services programming and facilities. Facility development, construction and acquisition are little different from those of the resource oriented agencies, except that much more programming occurs on and in the facilities. Secondly, the type of use will often differ between resource-oriented and human service administered areas.

Third, and most importantly, the human services agency concentrates on programs. The programs are intended to provide their clientel with opportunities for individual and group growth. David Gray and Seymour Greben in "Future Perspectives," a position paper for the National Recreation and Park Association, stated, "We must recognize the potential role of recreation in the development of people. The goals of organized recreation programs are to provide people opportunities for the exercise of their powers, opportunity for recreational experience, opportunity for the development of a positive self-image."

With the reduced funding levels of the Land and Water Conservation Fund, elimination of funding for the Urban Park and Recreation Recovery Act, and traditional state funds targeted for resource based agencies, those agencies who have a primary mission of human services have been effectively shut out of funding opportunities.

It was out of the belief that the quality of life of Central state residents could be positively affected by increased recreation opportunities, that legislation was proposed that will call for the creation of a "Central State Council on Recreation and Parks."

4. WHO:

TARGET AUDIENCE:
Who do we want to influence?

Legislative Level:

- Legislators on the Natural Resource Committee and Appropriations Committee in the House & Senate

- All legislators

5. HOW:

STRATEGY: What strategies can we use to reach our target groups and accomplish our goals?

STRATEGY 1

Convince legislators to support the creation of a Central State Council on Recreation and Parks. Make them aware of the importance of recreation and parks to the physical, social, mental and economic well being of the state.

• Strategic Message: The current funding for recreation and parks is declining and needs additional support.

• Strategic Message: A well maintained and financed public recreation and park system is essential to the quality of life of this state.

• Strategic Message: A high quality of life will retain business and industry, tourists, and residents and encourage new businesses, industry, tourists and residents.

Tactics for Strategy 1

A. Monitor the bill's progress. Assign one person to monitor the progress of the bill through the House and Senate committees.

B. Phone calls to legislators. Activate state legislative network to call legislators at key times prior to committee hearings and voting.

C. Letter-writing campaign. Monitor state natural resources committee progress and appropriations committee process and activate state legislative network to generate letters to legislators at crucial times.

D. Legislative visits. Plan a series of visits to key legislators by members, board members, council members, and supporters. Educate them about the need for a state resource for recreation and parks and find out how they plan to vote in committee and on appropriations.

E. Annual Convention. Invite the Chair of the Senate and/or House Natural Resources Committee to be the main speaker at the state's annual convention. Ask the Chair to speak on the chances of the "Council" legislation passing, and on potential funding.

F. Telephone Poll. Assign four members to call all state legislators, asking for their position on the proposed "Council." Research the amount of support for creating the "Council."

G. Educational/PR literature. Mail a packet of educational materials to legislators, with facts and figures about recreation and parks. Explain the association's position clearly.

H. Thank you letters. Send follow-up letters to legislators thanking them for their support.

STRATEGY 2

Make legislators aware of their own personal leisure ethic and motivations and how it has an impact on their lives.

• Strategic Message: Knowledge about personal leisure is integral part of daily life--stress response, mental health, relaxation, sense of perspective.

• Strategic Message: Good leisure ethic can be maintained through a proper understanding and commitment that is gained through public and private non-profit recreation opportunities.

• Strategic Message: Recreation and parks is a legitimate profession representing a discrete body of knowledge.

Tactics for Strategy 2

A. Legislative fitness and leisure day. Working with Central Association for Health, Physical Education, Recreation and Dance, hold a legislative fitness and leisure day allowing legislators to take leisure assessments and receive results and leisure counseling. Use recreation and park professionals to perform the tests.

B. News conference. Hold news conference to announce the leisure assessment, fitness and leisure day, etc. for legislators. Also distribute press releases, etc.

STRATEGY 3

Identify secondary and allied groups who can be motivated to influence legislators (i.e., parents, artists, travel and tourism, other professional associations, private non-profit organizations, sports organizations and clubs, etc.)

• Strategic Message: The opportunity for growth and additional funding in human services opportunities can grow if you will support a Council on Recreation and Parks.

• Strategic Message: The future of the state's recreation, park, and human services opportunities may be stagnant or reduced. You need to let your legislator know you are for the "Council."

Tactics for Strategy 3

A. Coordinate activities. Assign state public communications coordinator to monitor and coordinate activities.

B. Speakers bureau. To reach influential state and community leaders, organize a statewide speaker's bureau from membership to speak to professional and civic groups about the need for a Council on Recreation and Parks.

C. Press lunches. To reach community leaders and others, plan one monthly press lunch around the state in four major cities to educate reporters about recreation and parks. Provide "background" information as well as specifics on the current legislation.

D. "Key influencer" breakfasts. To reach influential individuals in the state, hold three "key influencer" breakfasts throughout the state to discuss the need for coalition building, cooperation and sommon goals, as well as the administrators, area political leaders, appropriate business leaders, and other representatives of allied groups.

E. Radio appearances. Plan six radio appearances by newsworthy and/or knowledgeable individuals concentrated three months before the committee vote. Spots will be targeted to home districts of the natural resource and appropriations committees members and the state capital. Use the telephone tree to alert "key influencers" and legislative "fence-sitters" to listen tothe interview shows.

F. Resolutions from allied organizations. Make contact with allied organizations, make presentations to their appropriate board of directors and secure resolutions from each organization. Insure that they mail the resolutions directly to legislators. Encourage each organization to prepare a press release to coincide with adoption of the resolution. Keep copies of the resolution as part of a press kit.

name _Martin Blaufach, President_

association _Central State AHPERD_

Target Audience
1. _Legislators or Appropriation Cmte._
2. _All Legislators_
• Level _State_   • Branch _Legislature_

For Strategy No. _One_

Objective: _Retain the current mandate for PE K-12_

Strategies:

1. _Convince legislators to maintain PE requirement by keeping it_
as a separate budget line item. Make them aware of the
importance of physical education.

2. _Make legislators aware of their own personal health_
and well-being.

3. _Identify secondary target groups which can be_
motivated to influence legislators.

Target Audience _Legislative_

Strategy _Convince Legislators to maintain PE requirement_

Tactics:	Personnel	Resources	Miscellaneous
WHAT _Educational/ PR Information_ **WHEN** _December - February_ **WHERE** _University Hall_	_To Mark, Pete, Fred, Mary Ann, Leslie, plus Leslie's majors Class Proj._	1. _printing + postage at $10,000 from PREH funds._ 2. _University PR Dept. will design + write FREE._ 3. _Leslie's majors to address/stuff envelopes_	_Mark will get final detailed budget_ _Jo will approve all copy and design, coordinate and keep on schedule_
WHAT _Annual Convention_ **WHEN** _June 20-24_ **WHERE** _Collegetown_	_Martin will write and invite Chairs of House & Senate Conservation Committee_	1. _Use college copies, postage & secretarial support_	_Martin needs to get Mary Ann to know about guests before Aug 20th for program printing._

Impacting on Recreation and Park Legislation

43

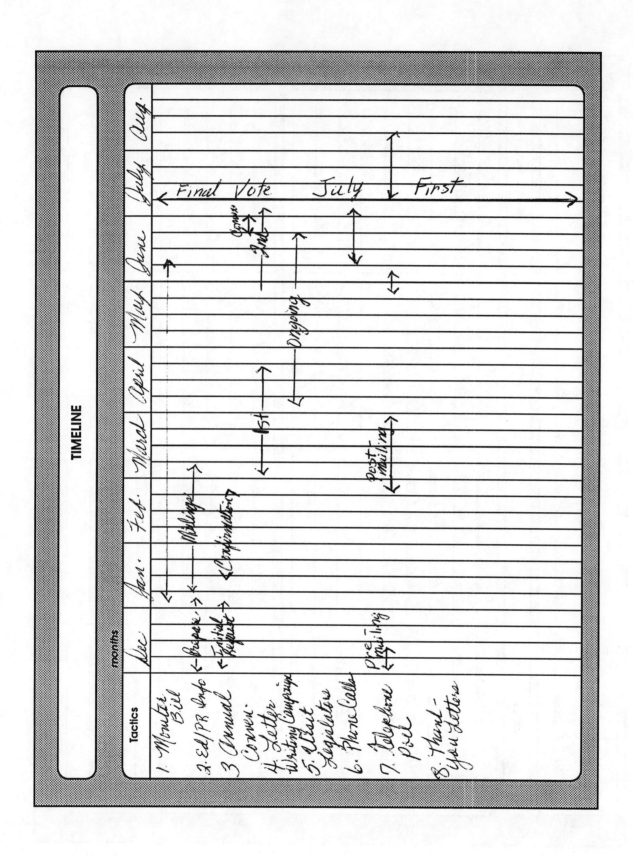

5

Legislative Tools

Why Legislation is Passed

Legislation is passed for many different and complex reasons, but all legislation is passed because a majority of legislators vote for it. Legislators choose to vote for particular bills.

- The legislator truly believes that the bill will benefit the public and is in the public good.
- The legislator personally disagrees with the bill, but thinks most constituents favor it. Although the legislator does not plan to work hard to get the bill passed, voting for it will produce good press back home.
- The legislator thinks that the bill generates little constituent interest, but political party leaders are calling in the help given during the last election by asking for a yes vote. Voting for the bill seems a fairly innocuous way of repaying "political capitol" without hurting his or her image with district voters.
- The legislator knows district voters are against the bill but feels personally bound to support it. Knowing it will hurt reelection chances, but placing personal integrity first, the lawmakers takes the risk and votes for the bill.
- The legislator thinks that most district voters are against the bill, but a main campaign contributor is asking for an affirmative vote. Believing that the bad press can be overcome with a strong Public Relations campaign, and knowing that the next election can't be won without the contributor's money, he votes yes.
- The legislator knows that the bill responds to a very volatile issue over which district constituents are evenly divided. Having held numerous hearings around the district to determine what voters want, the legislator votes for the legislation, but introduces a series of amendments to significantly weaken offensive portions of the bill, hoping to gain the support of both sides, and thereby represent all district constituents.

These situations could apply to any legislator. Each bill is different; each vote has unique variables. Legislators weigh many considerations before deciding how to vote. Constituents, a primary consideration, are not the only consideration. Sometimes the weight their opinion holds depends on the strength they display. Loyalties often conflict. Obeying is not an exact science. The bottom line--the outcome--depends on legislators, who, like other people, are often unpredictable.

When faced with a new bill, a legislator has options,

- vote for it
- vote against it
- offer amendments to it
- stay home.

The last option is often used as a way of offending no one in the face of conflicting loyalties. The political game is much like other games. The legislative player can play offense or defense, change the play offering amendments, or sit on the bench. Sometimes no move is the wisest move of all. In each situation there are judgement calls, consideration of which play to use, which players, when to call time out, and when to bring in special teams. As the game is played, the nuances become more evident, and players become more proficient. The basic rules are only the beginning. Subtleties of the game that really count. While playing, watch, listen, and learn.

Legislator's Information Sources

A legislator must balance all these forces and come up with the best decision. The first step is to get the best and most current information about an issue, and then to seek good advice. Legislators receive advise from many quarters.
- Personal staff
- Committee staff
- Study groups, working groups, or special caucuses
- Party platforms and position papers
- District sources, such as newspapers, local party officials
- Special interest groups
- National, state, and local media
- Executive branch executives, resources, agencies, study papers
- Constituent and public input--hearings, testimony, constituent letters
- Other members
- House/senate floor debate
- Personal study

The wealth of information available often exceeds time and attention needed to process it. Legislators must filter available information They must screen the information according to its source. A legislator might decide that certain in-nation sources are unreliable, biased, or incomplete. Others are consistently late, unintelligible, too academic, or difficult to understand. Legislators quickly learn which resources are reliable and which are a waste of time. Be a good, clear, timely, accurate, and reliable source of information for the legislator.

How Legislators Decide to Vote

After gathering information, a legislator decides what action (or reaction) to take. Legislators must take positions of low profile or high visibility. They can be leaders, reasoning negotiators, menders of intraparty feuds, or hardliners.

How legislators move depends on who they are and how they think. It can depend on personal history and value systems, profession, the progress of a career as a legislator, age, position in the party, family, business interests, hobbies ,and lifestyle. Here are some questions which legislators might consider prior to a vote.
- They must decide how legislation will benefit their constituents, or their districts.
- They must consider whether they will benefit by association with the legislation.
- They must consider whether there be a political or public backlash.
- They must weigh the legislations potential for controversy.
- They must discover which of their colleagues support the legislation.
- They must consider the party's position.
- They must consider the governor's position.
- They must decide whether the legislation will benefit the state.
- They must consider the cost of supporting the legislation.
- They must decide whether the legislation is necessary, and if so, what is wrong with the status quo.
- Legislators must decide who will benefit by a piece of legislation, and who it favors.
- They must find out who supports it.
- They must find out who is against it.

- They must define the public attitude toward the legislation. A well-respected issue will have firm public support.
- Legislators need to try to measure outcome, to know what signs will tell them the bill is successful.

Legislators operate on political outcome and need to be assured of the bill's place in the political climate. A good advocate can reassure the legislator about the political as well as educational, social, or physical benefits of a bill.

Lobbying

To lobby means to influence or persuade public officials to take a desired action, to pass (or defeat) legislation. An effective lobbyist is convincing and persuasive at selling an idea. The word, lobby, which was formerly slang, suggests persons waiting in halls or lobbies to talk with legislators. A lobbyist's effectiveness today still depends on being at the right place at the right time. Timing and knowledge are critical to an effective lobbyist.

Most professional lobbyists don't really sell influence, but access. Because they know the system, are familiar with individuals involved in the process, and are located at the capitol, they can get an issue heard. Access to the political system, however, is available to everyone. A broker is not necessary. Everyone has the right to give federal, state, and local representatives their ideas about a public issue. Communicating with a representative, whether by letter, phone, or in person, is the most accessible way to participate in government between elections.

Most People Do Not Participate

Of all the eligible voters in the United States, only 51%in the 1988 presidential election. That means that President Bush was elected by less than 27% of the total eligible voters. Although voting to choose who will govern is considered a rare and unparalleled privilege in most parts of the world today, Americans use it little and take it for granted.

Lobbyists and groups who lobby can be effective because so few citizens care enough about their government to get involved. Lack of interest and involvement by everyday citizens contributes to keeping professional lobbyists successful. No matter how much money an individual or business has contributed to a campaign, politicians are still elected by a majority of the voters in their districts.

A politician's livelihood depends on knowing the needs and desires of his constituents, and keeping them reasonably content, if not happy, with his performance. Politicians have a keen and personal interest in hearing from their constituents. They are predisposed to listen.

Political Capital

Some legislators must be persuaded to vote for recreation and park programs. Lobbyists enter the politician's world and ask for something. Politicians may not do as they are asked simply because it is the right thing to do. They may expect something in return. Prepare a map for this obstacle course. Although the way cannot always be mapped out ahead of time, some signposts have been left by those who went before.

Play to win. Half-hearted efforts waste time. Legislation campaigns take everyone's time, money, energy, cooperation, and patience. Don't start without a commitment.

Assume the campaign will take a long time, and develop an impeccable reputation. Because legislative grapevines active, always deliver on any promise on time. Promise to get any requested information, and then follow through. Make sure any dates are the best available. Talk positively about issues, rather than negatively about the opposition. Always present a consistent, professional image.

Always try to be bipartisan. Most political issues can be attributed to one political party or the other. Tuition tax credits, tax reductions, and a strong national defense are platforms of the Republican party. Women's rights, student aid grants, and arms reduction treaties are issues most often associated with the Democratic party. In general, if an issue is associated with one party, it may fare well when the party is in power, but not when the opposition holds the power. Recreation and parks issues can appeal to everyone. If both parties accept an issue, effective lobbying efforts can be successful, no matter who wins an election.

Learn how to use political capital. Political capital is the name one political observer has given to the legal tender of political bargaining. Political capital can be publicity, the ability to get political contributions or speaking engagements, the respect of colleagues, influence with the executive branch, or any other commodity that can be used by a legislator. Political capital can be imagined as an almost tangible form of exchange upon which political bartering and law making depends.

Learn to trade in political capital. Try to boost the legislator who offers to introduce a bill to support recreation and parks issues. Legislators need public support just as much as citizens need legislative support.

Voters

Any association has what legislators want most--voters. Associations consist of a defined population of organized and politically active professionals. If membership is large and the organization is active, membership support could possible tip the scales in a close election. In addition, because many members are in the public school system, they see parents, other teachers, and community professionals daily. They have access to a secondary audience of voters.

Find out about members and sell them on a selected issue. They are mostly college educated, mid-income level, eligible voters. Find out how many of them are registered to vote. Conduct a survey to discover their ages, how many people they see every week, and how much money they contribute to the state economy annually. Find out how many of them voted in the last election, how many volunteered in a political campaign (of either party) how many contributed at least some money to a political candidate in the last election, and how many belong to other influential groups.

If membership is on the rise, do a graph that shows a trend of increasing membership. Take a membership poll at the next state or district convention. Do a random sample, or mail out survey forms with the next membership renewal form. Know the membership as any association's primary strength and power.

Respectability

All politicians want to be known. Legislators make many controversial choices which don't have a positive public relations value. Health, wellness, fitness, and recreation and parks issues carry a reputation of being respectable, wholesome, and good. Supporting a respectable cause can, in the eyes of the public, enhance a politician's image.

Publicity

Publicity gives a representative exposure, and the possibility of a wider audience, more votes, perhaps even a higher position in the government. Speaking engagements also give exposure and possibly a substantial fee. Political contributions provide buying exposure via campaign ads, mailers, and fund raisers. Election to public office requires exposure to the public. Politicians want to be known, liked and respected. Most of all, they want to be elected and reelected.

Publicity means exposure to the voters which means more votes. Publicity can be the most effective political capital. Even legislators are often hard pressed to come up with real news, and editors ignore self-serving news releases designed to keep the legislator before the public. Give a legislator an issue which is news with a positive, respectable image, and make an opportunity for positive media exposure. Politicians always look for an appealing issue. Legislators can often generate their own media exposure, but their staffs are small. As a courtesy for their support, offer to generate publicity for a joint venture. Work closely with the press office, and be sure to send the legislator copies of all media materials. Handling the media successfully will be appreciated by the legislator and will contribute to any organization's reputation. Gain the legislator's respect, and ensure that media focus is on the issue and not only the legislator (See Tools for the Media).

Political Endorsement

By courting them, legislators often hope to get special interest group endorsement during elections. Political endorsements signify a whole new category of political activism, but if an organization is ready for it, a candidate who has been particularly helpful may be endorsed.

Campaigns

For an individual, contributing money to election campaigns is certainly acceptable. For an organization, it can become complicated. Organizational donations to election campaigns for politicians are regulated by strict federal and state laws and regulations. PACs (Political Action Committees) are often formed, separate from parent organizations if nonprofits wish to encourage group political activity. Otherwise an organization should not use this form of political capital.

Monitoring Legislation

Applying the right amount of pressure at the right time is the secret of a successful legislative campaign. Pinpointing the correct moment to apply pressure depends on knowing where a bill is in the legislative process at all times. Being able to understand and track bills through the legislative process is essential to lobbying.

Where to Get Information

Do some preliminary research before approaching a legislator. Start at the local public library or college library. Each state has a "Blue Book," usually published by the clerk of the senate or the secretary of state, which contains general information about the state and its government and a directory of state offices and officials (executive and judicial branch). Although each state chooses different material to go into its blue book, state blue books may contain:
- Statistics about the state (population, economics, demographics, history)
- State constitution
- County structure and statistics
- Municipal structure and statistics
- State revenue sources, and expenditures
- Political party structure and officials
- List of state legislators and a short biography of each
- State departmental statistics
- Advisory, licensing, planning, and governing boards and councils
- Federal offices located within the state
- Educational institutions, statistics, and officials.

The state Chamber of Commerce also publishes an excellent source book for each state, with information which may be missing from the blue book. If these resources are not available or do not contain all the needed information, ask the librarian where to find answers to the following questions.
- The number of state senators and representatives
- The term of office of state senators and representatives
- When the legislature meets
- A map of the state legislative districts
- A description of each political district, including economic, political, industrial, educational, health, and demographic data
- The number of standing committees and subcommittees there are in the house
- The number of standing committees and subcommittees there are in the senate

- Information on any special caucuses or ad hoc committees
- Information on the political party that controls the house and the senate
- The name of the speaker of the house
- The name of the president of the senate and the president pro tem
- The names of the local senator and representative, and a short biography of each
- A local source for bills which have been introduced

Two other good sources of information on the political process are the state and local chapters of the League of Women Voters and Common Cause.

Ask a Representative

After exhausting available resources, call a representative. Each representative obtains information, acting as a conduit from the government to the citizen. Much of a legislator's staff time, on the national and state levels, involves "case work," helping constituents with individual problems. Intelligent inquiries can help establish a credible relationship.

Tracking the Bill

Tracking the bill through the legislature is necessary to a legislative campaign. Here again, states differ. Check with local legislators. Some states have "bill rooms" which distribute copies of bills that have been introduced. Ask a state legislator for its location and procedures. Often the Rules Committee puts out daily calendars which show legislation to be acted on. The state legislator may also put out a status sheet which lists where all bills are in legislation. Subscribe to the state capitol newspaper to keep up to date.

By far, the best source is a legislator and his personal or committee staff. Once a bill has been introduced and referred to committee, a phone call to the committee staff can pinpoint its status. Such contact develops relationships with committee staffers. At crucial times, daily phone calls may be needed.

If the membership is organized as suggested in the Getting Started section, the Lobbying Task Force acts primarily to track the bill. After the bill is introduced, they will need to know when and if the bill will be called up before the committee, and when and if public hearings are planned. If the committee schedules public hearings, note who will choose spokespersons to testify. If the committee chair will decide, find out which legislative network members are active in his district. Decide what sort of pressure can be applied. The game has begun.

Legislative Tracking Chart

There are several tools which may help monitor legislation. The first is a Legislative Tracking Chart (Figure 5.1). It is particularly helpful if work is going on several bills at once. It helps keep track of where the bill is in the legislative process. A Legislative Tracking Chart can also be set up like the Vote Tally Chart (Figure 5.2).

Keep Members Informed

Keep members informed with bulletins about proposed legislation and legislation in process. Include a hotline to provide a sort of "telephone tree" through which concerned citizens can voice their opinions to officials.

Legislative Tracking Chart	
Bill No. _____	Bill No. _____
Title _____	Title _____
Sponsor _____	Sponsor _____
Co-Sponsors _____	Co-Sponsors _____
Date Introduced _____	Date Introduced _____
Committee Referred to _____	Committee Referred to _____
Committee Chairman _____	Committee Chairman _____
Subcommittee Referred to _____	Subcommittee Referred to _____
Subcommittee Chairman _____	Subcommittee Chairman _____
Date of Committee Hearings _____	Date of Committee Hearings _____
Date of Committee Consideration _____	Date of Committee Consideration _____
Placed on House/Senate Calendar (date) ___	Placed on House/Senate Calendar (date) ___
Second Reading _____	Second Reading _____
Third Reading _____	Third Reading _____
1st House Consideration	***2nd House Consideration***

Figure 5.1 Legislative Tracking Chart

Sample: Legislative Bulletin

IOWA
PARK & RECREATION ASSOCIATION

Legislative Bulletin

Legislative Chairperson - Dan McLean - 319-398-5065
2000 Mt. Vernon Road SE, Cedar Rapids, IA 52403
January 19, 1990

State Legislation

Pool Rules

The 1990 Governor's Budget allows for $134,000 and 4 staff members in expenditures by the Department of Health for administration of the swimming pool inspection program. This is based on projected revenue of $300,000. The Health Department requested a budget of $300,000 and 8 staff members to administer the program. <u>The net effect is to use monies designated for swimming pool inspection for other state programs</u>.

What are the ramifications of this budget recommendation? **First**, the fees for the program must be paid NLT 1 May 1990 (assuming the rules are accepted by the Legislative Rules Committee). Fees will be sent to the state unless your county has been certified to do inspections. **Second**, even though your fees may be paid (which also pays for the inspection) you are not protected against claims until you aquatic facility has been inspected and certified by the state. That means, you could pay fees and not receive the protection the Iowa League built into the original bill.

The rules will return to the legislative rules committee on February 5. Prior to that time you need to contact your legislator to let him know that the governor's office is potentially denying you a service your are "required" to pay for. Encourage them to amend the budget to include the appropriate funding level. If this is unsuccessful we will use the legislative hot-line to encourage you to attend a meeting of the legislative rules committee to oppose implementation of the rules.

Discipline and Dismissal

SF (Senate File) 389 adds <u>Disciple and Dismissal</u> to the list of mandatory issues for negotiations under Chapter 20, the state's Collective Bargaining Act. In the Iowa League's January 12 (No. 1) <u>Action Call</u>, this issue is discussed in detail. Please review the publication and provide your legislator with appropriate input. If you do not receive copies, your clerk or city manager should.

REAP

The municipal review committee for REAP has been appointed. Joe Stevens (Ames) and Steve Wyatt (Decorah) have been asked to serve. Joe will serve as chairperson of the review committee.

Legislative Hot -Line

The Legislative Hot-Line has been updated and is provided herein. If you see corrections, please let me know. (319-398-5065)

Legislative Telephone Numbers

To reach your legislator, while in sessic.. please use the following numbers:
> House - 515-281-3221
> Senate - 515-281-3371

Sample: IPRA Legislative "Hotline"

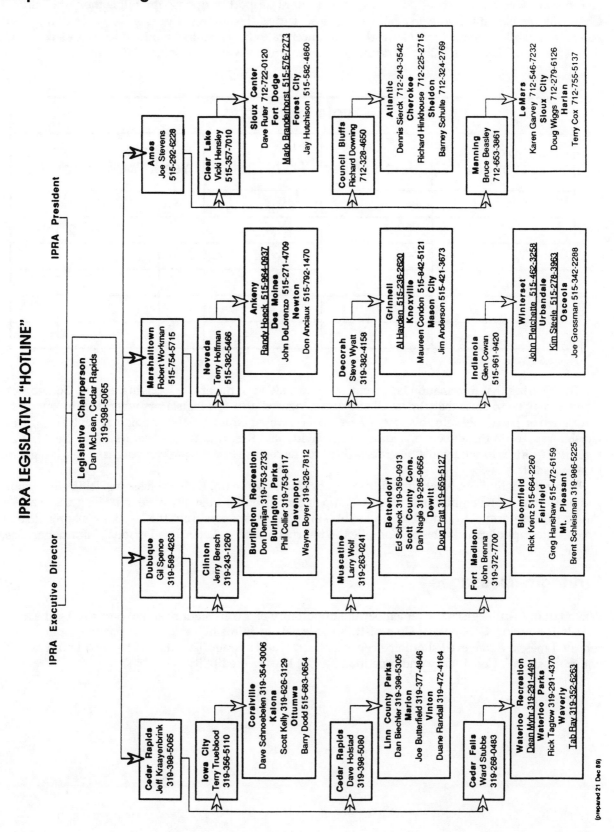

IPRA LEGISLATIVE "HOTLINE"

IPRA President

IPRA Executive Director

Legislative Chairperson
Dan McLean, Cedar Rapids
319-398-5065

Ames
Joe Stevens
515-292-6228

Clear Lake
Vicki Hensley
515-357-7010

Sioux Center
Dave Ruter 712-722-0120
Fort Dodge
Marlo Branderhorst 515-576-7273
Forest City
Jay Hutchison 515-582-4860

Council Bluffs
Richard Downing
712-328-4650

Atlantic
Dennis Sierck 712-243-3542
Cherokee
Richard Hinkhouse 712-225-2715
Sheldon
Barney Schulte 712-324-2769

Manning
Bruce Beasley
712-653-3861

LeMars
Karen Garvey 712-546-7232
Sioux City
Doug Wiggs 712-279-6126
Harlan
Terry Cox 712-755-5137

Marshalltown
Robert Workman
515-754-5715

Nevada
Terry Hoffman
515-382-5466

Ankeny
Randy Hoeck 515-964-0937
Des Moines
John DeLorenzo 515-271-4709
Newton
Don Anciaux 515-792-1470

Decorah
Steve Wyatt
319-382-4158

Grinnell
Al Hayden 515-236-2620
Knoxville
Maureen Condon 515-842-5121
Mason City
Jim Anderson 515-421-3673

Indianola
Glen Cowan
515-961-9420

Winterset
John Pletchette 515-462-3258
Urbandale
Kim Steele 515-278-3963
Osceola
Joe Grossman 515-342-2288

Dubuque
Gil Spence
319-589-4263

Clinton
Jerry Bersch
319-243-1260

Burlington Recreation
Don Demian 319-753-2733
Burlington Parks
Phil Collier 319-753-8117
Davenport
Wayne Boyer 319-326-7812

Muscatine
Larry Wolf
319-263-0241

Bettendorf
Ed Scheck 319-359-0913
Scott County Cons.
Dan Nagle 319-285-9656
Dewitt
Doug Pratt 319-659-5127

Fort Madison
John Brenna
319-372-7700

Bloomfield
Rick Krenz 515-664-2260
Fairfield
Greg Harshaw 515-472-6159
Mt. Pleasant
Brent Schleisman 319-986-5225

Cedar Rapids
Jeff Kraayenbrink
319-398-5065

Iowa City
Terry Trueblood
319-356-5110

Coralville
Dave Schnoebelen 319-354-3006
Kalona
Scott Kelly 319-626-3129
Ottumwa
Barry Dodd 515-683-0654

Cedar Rapids
Dave Holstad
319-398-5080

Linn County Parks
Dan Biechler 319-398-5305
Marion
Joe Butterfield 319-377-4846
Vinton
Duane Randall 319-472-4164

Cedar Falls
Ward Stubbs
319-268-0483

Waterloo Recreation
Dean Mohr 319-291-4491
Waterloo Parks
Rick Tagtow 319-291-4370
Waverly
Tab Ray 319-352-6263

(prepared 21 Dec 89)

Vote Tally Chart

Another aid which can be useful in tracking legislators support or oppose the bill is the Vote Tally Chart (Figure 5.2). If the vote on a bill will be close, a careful counting of yeas and nays can project an outcome, and allow Grass Roots Networkers to concentrate efforts on uncommitted legislators who could decide the vote. The Vote Tally Chart can focus on where pressure may be needed most.

Vote Tally Chart					
Legislator & Staffer	Phone No.	Party District	Projected Vote		
			Yes	Undeciced	No

Figure 5.2 Vote Tally Chart

By ensuring that information is current, these two aids can maximize lobbying efforts. Sometimes the vote may be so close that almost all efforts are focused on a few legislators who serve in key committee or party roles. In this case, target a concentrated educational campaign at several legislators. To do this effectively, know the individuals. Research the legislators. Ask the legislators' offices to send you a biography (kept for media use and during campaigns). This is a good place to start.

From there, find out what committees the legislators serve on, their professions, legislative tenure, and main campaign contributors. Election campaign contributions usually have to be filed and made public. This information should be easy to obtain. Old newspapers from the legislator's home district or the state capitol can also help. Compile the information on a Legislator Personal Information Sheet (Figure 5.3).

Strategic Messages

When talking with legislators, remember the importance of a consistent message outlined by the Legislative Action Committee. On a visit to the legislator in his home district or at the capitol, the repeated message conveyed should be consistent, clear, and strong. Threats and hysteria brand a nonprofessional. Consistency and repetition are the keys to credibility.

Legislator Personal Information Sheet

Name _____

Party _____

Capitol Address _____

Capitol Phone _____

Home District Address _____

Home District Phone _____

Personal

Age _____ Marital Status _____

Family

Spouse's Name _____ Age _____

Children _____ Age(s) _____

_____

Family History _____

_____

Religion _____

Occupation _____

Financial Intersts/Income/Business Interests

_____

Educational Background _____

_____

Social Clubs-Civic Groups (Legislator/Spouse)

_____

Political

Party _____

Previous Elected Offices _____

Political History _____

_____

_____

_____

Date First Elected to Legislature _____

Opponent in Last Election _____

Margin of Victory _____

Primary Campaign Contributors _____

_____

_____

_____

Endorsed Candidacy? Campaign? _____

_____

Legislative

Committee Assignments _____

_____

Number of Years in Legislature _____

Major Leadership Positions/Caucuses _____

_____

_____

Figure 5.3 Legislator Personal Information Sheet

6

Lobbying Techniques

Sponsors and Cosponsors

Although only legislators introduce a bill, sometimes two or more legislators, called cosponsors, jointly introduce the same bill. A bill may have several cosponsors.

In some states, legislators may be allowed to sign on as cosponsors after the bill has been introduced. Signing on as cosponsors is a way of demonstrating support. Many legislators are able to take credit for a popular bill by being a cosponsor. Cosponsorship signifies more than just an affirmative vote. It implies credit for the creation of the bill and indicates much stronger support. If a state allows cosponsors, recruiting them is a good way to prove wide-based support. Direct some lobbying activities toward gathering cosponsor sign-ons.

Dear Colleague Letters

Dear colleague letters are frequently used at the congressional level to push for passage of proposed legislation. The term refers to a letter from one legislator to another, urging support for or against a bill. It is really a form of internal or congressional lobbying in which legislators lobby each other. A letter from another legislator or colleague will carry more weight than a letter from a special interest group. Ask some influential legislators, who have shown support to an issue, to write a "Dear Colleague" letter to a committee holdout, preferably from the same political party.

Coalitions

Another technique for demonstrating support for a legislative initiative is to join with other organizations to form a coalition. Coalitions are usually formed around a single issue or set of issues on which the coalition members agree. Coalition member organizations are usually similar in scope, (e.g., all state level organizations, all national level organizations) who maintain their independence, agreeing only to work together on one issue. Coalitions can exist over time or they can be temporary, and are often informal in organizational structure.

A coalition, by increasing number and type of individual supporters, demonstrates broader support than a single issue group. The coalition functions as a coordinating body to disseminate information, reduce overhead communication costs by reducing the number of people who gather information directly from the capital, and share information and resources.

Two essentials for all coalitions, however, are participation and independence. An organization cannot participate in a coalition only to receive information without also contributing either, time, information, or resources. Member organizations can contribute in a variety of ways if money is in short supply.

Coalition member organizations often jealously guard their independence. Although temporarily united for a common goal, they might shift political sides of the fence tomorrow. More lasting coalitions can develop their own identities, slowly and over time, the way other organizations do, and become powerful. Coalitions also take the pressure off one organization, while all member organizations band together with each other in a common effort.

In looking for coalition member groups, consider well-respected and influential state organizations. Be careful that the organization is not used to support something which it does not favor. Remember, coalitions are formed for a single issue on an ad hoc basis. While information and resources need to be shared, make sure there is an even exchange. An organization is not obligated to support issues outside the scope of the coalition. Make sure that coalition relationships are clearly established at the beginning. Many groups have similar interests in most communities and states.

Support Statements

Another way to gather support from other organizations without forming a coalition is to ask them to endorse a bill or recreation and parks in general. Often groups such as the Association of Retarded Citizens, the local Red Cross, sports and recreation clubs and associations, and civic groups will be glad to endorse health, wellness, fitness, and recreation and parks knowledge and skills. The best way to get endorsements from other organizations is to research the organization and write a resolution that meets a goal, but also fits it into their philosophy. They will almost surely change wording, but they will find it easier to change what has already been written than to write something from scratch. Chances of actually getting their endorsement increase.

Community and Civic Groups

Community and civic groups are not only great local sources of support, but also good information disseminators. Civic groups allow access to a network of community leaders, citizens, and professionals which members may not ordinarily know. Civic groups can help people who do not work in government, and who may never have thought about recreation and parks issues. Civic groups can expand an organizations' reach. Ask them for a support statement, speak before one of their weekly meetings, or provide them with informational material about recreation and parks issues (See the Resource section for a list of civic groups).

Community and civic groups can be very useful to the Grass Roots Network, garnering community support and letting legislators know that the district supports recreation and parks issues. They also have access to legislators, may of whom are members of their groups. Community and civic groups can be solicited by the Finance Task Force for donations to defray some of the costs of operating a legislative campaign.

Personal Endorsements

Getting personal endorsement from VIPs can influence legislators. A VIP can be almost anyone who is influential in the community, is perceived as influential, or who has the ear of a legislator. Personal endorsements can come from participants, part-time staff, mayors, politicians, recreation and park board members, the legislator's next door neighbor, or a major campaign donor.

Find out where the legislator and/or his family participate in recreation and parks activities. Any members who know a legislator personally could arrange meetings at which issues can be discussed. Consider the following when seeking personal endorsements:
- Campaign contributors, workers and volunteers (campaign reports are usually filed with the State Secretary of State)
- Colleagues and business associates (check press clippings, official biography, *Who's Who*, professional associations and boards, business boards, stockholders)
- Friends (check membership in the civic groups, clubs, PTAs, college alumni, arts councils)
- Political colleagues (former congressmen, legislators, mayors, party activists, local politicians, city councilmen, school board members)
- Educational leaders, (university presidents, principals)
- Religious leaders

- Labor and business leaders (board of trade, chamber of commerce, industry recruitment committees, tourist boards)
- Local state and national celebrities (entertainers, Olympic athletes, the winning college basketball coach)

Testimony and Public Hearings

Public response to proposed legislation is often requested through public hearings. Public hearings are also held for executive branch or administrative reasons, such as changes in administrative rules or regulations, or curriculum changes proposed by a board of education. Often, those holding the hearings will attempt to get as many different interest groups involved as possible in presenting testimony. It is usually politically safer to seek advice and then not follow it, than not seek it at all.

Perception and illusion are important political tools. President Reagan asked the National Governor's Association what they thought of his block grant proposals because he knew they favored the concept. Although he probably did ask their opinion as he was formulating the plan, this public request for input was really a political public relations device, intended to publicize support, not gather diverse opinions. When the Reagan Department of Education proposed rules to change the P.L. 94-142 regulations, public input, through the normal regulation review process, was so strong that they withdrew proposed regulations. Changing federal regulations, a process described by law, is open to everyone, and is therefore less subject to political manipulation than other processes, such as curriculum changes by a curriculum committee, or local school board decisions. Be aware of the legal requirements for public input, and political games being played.

Public hearings and agendas are scheduled in advance, and individuals requesting to testify usually do so in writing through the legislative committee staff. An active Grass Roots Network in the committee chairman's district can help place an individual on the agenda.

It is often helpful to solicit other groups with a similar message to testify. Hearing support from recreation and park professionals can be interpreted as self-serving; hearing it from the local ARC, private non profit associations, and civic clubs shows broad public support. Get as many members to testify as possible, If the committee is seeking broad representation, find out who is testifying for other groups. Convince them to put in a good word for recreation and parks issues.

Don't be afraid to show illustrations when testifying. The use of charts and graphs is common, but be more creative if it would be appropriate. Large mounted photos of faces of participants in recreation and park programs might be effective. Strike a creative in your approach to visiting with legislators at a public hearing. Check with the Lobbying Task Force to see what is appropriate. Because of constant contact with legislators and staff at the capitol, the task force members have an idea of what would be acceptable and what would be received negatively. Make sure those organizing the hearing are well informed. Don't forget to invite the press.

Events

Education influences legislators. Like education, events can define the profession and demonstrate political power. One such event is the Legislative Fitness and Leisure Day, which several state associations have held successfully working in cooperation with their state association for health, physical education, recreation and dance. Providing legislators with a variety of individualized health and leisure days has successfully educated legislators about the need for professional recreation and park practitioners. Events should coincide with legislative votes, but this is often not possible due to the unpredictability of the legislative session. With proper reminders, legislators could keep recreation and parks matters in mind from the start. In addition to leisure days, consider a Legislative Run, Legislative Olympics, or other events that will make legislators aware of recreation and parks issues, and to publicize the association. Show commitment by holding these events at the same time as the annual convention at the state capitol. Be a visible force to the legislature. Be creative. Think about what would make good television news footage.

Publicity

Don't forget publicity is a lobbying technique. Remember that legislators serve in a public arena. Their political livelihood depends on the whims of the public. Publicity is important in legislative campaigns because it can
- help garner constituent support
- help "create a public issue"
- be used as "political capital"
- demonstrate public support and keep the issue before the public (See Tools for the Media for specific information)

Constituents' Mail Gets Read

Obviously, some of the these methods are not feasible for state associations. Study show that spontaneous or orchestrated mail has a real and powerful impact on staffers. Large corporations, unions, and political action committees can give money to campaigns, but individuals write a legislator's paycheck and decide whether or not to keep him on the job. Remember, the legislator's best interest lies in monitoring the pulse of his district on every issue. Let him know that the organization's stand echos that pulse.

Form Letters

Orchestrated letter writing campaigns or form letters do have an impact. Although they are often readily identifiable as "orchestrated" by a state or national organization, and thus do not carry the same weight as a spontaneous response from the public at large, they do show that an organization has a large and vocal membership in the legislator's district that should not be ignored. Form letters do not go unnoticed. Use form letters with discretion. Let the situation determine what is best. Form letters are better than no letters, or individual responses which arrive too late.

Another approach used recently at the national level is printed postcards. The ultimate form letter, printed post cards can be distributed in recreation centers and parks, sporting goods stores, or left with local banks and merchants. They contain a printed message and require only the name and address of the district's legislator (usually supplied nearby) and a signature. Even the postage can be supplied. This approach was used by the banking industry to overturn legislation which required banks to deduct taxes from depositors' interest payments and forward them to the federal government—one of the most successful legislative campaigns in recent years. The post cards made it easy for many people to respond and by using the banks as distribution point for the post cards, a wide audience was alerted to the issue. Public input greatly enhanced the work of the powerful banking lobby in Washington. Although many congressman were incensed with this approach, the bankers won and the legislation was overturned. It was not a traditional approach, but it became a successful one.

Visits to Legislatures

Make a personal visit to a legislator to communicate views on an issue. For an important legislative issue, make a special trip to the capitol. If the issue is not at the crisis stage, wait until the legislator returns home. Some state legislators have offices in their districts, and most have specified times during which they make themselves available in schools, public libraries, or other public places to allow constituents to communicate their ideas and opinions. Make sure that at least one member attends each such session, or that at least one member visits legislators during legislative recess, to communicate the strategic message, take them background materials, keep them informed of the local issues surrounding recreation and parks, educate them about the need for more funding and quality programs, and demonstrate political interest and power.

If possible, hold state wide conventions at the capitol, and invite legislative leaders as keynote speakers. Show them that the organization is professionally and politically active, and a force to be considered when public policy decisions are made. Set a day aside for members to visit their legislators with information about proposed legislation, recreation and parks, and the association.

Phone Calls

Phone calls are another excellent way of communicating district voter support for a bill. Although they are costly, they are effective if well timed. Phone calls are most effective when used the day before a crucial committee of floor vote. When undecided or wavering in support, a flood of telephone calls from district voters can sway the legislator to make the right decision. Although phone calls are usually accepted by staff members, be assured that they communicate the pro and con numbers to their legislative bosses. Don't discount the use of phone calls or other forms of communication, such as mailgrams or hand delivered messages. When well placed, they can deliver the needed edge for a legislative victory.

Sample: Letter to a Legislator

*for health,
physical education,
recreation
and dance*

American Alliance © est. 1885

1900 Association Drive   Reston, Virginia   (703) 476-3400

August 3, 1983

The Honorable Senator Robert T. Stafford
625 Hart Senate Office Building
Washington D.C. 20510

Dear Senator Stafford:

I understand from Skip Vallee that the Subcommittee on Education, Arts
and Humanities plans to hold hearings in September on the findings and
recommendations of the Commission on Excellence in Education. Of the
three planned hearings, one will be available to Secretary Bell; one
will be available to state governors. I understand that the agenda
for the third hearing is not yet set. I would like to request that
the American Alliance be placed on the agenda for the third hearing.

The American Alliance is a national membership organization of over
45,000 educators in the fields of health, physical education, recreation and dance. Our members cover a broad spectrum, including
elementary school physical education teachers, university deans,
coaches, dance teachers, and community recreation leaders. They all
have the common commitment to educating our nation's children about
their physical health and wellbeing.

The American Alliance is concerned that the Commission's report has
neglected the disciplines which we represent. Although physical
education and health education are integral to the public school
curriculum, their current or future place in the schools was not
mentioned. We believe there is a role for our disciplines in the
plan for excellence in education. We think it is especially important
that the subcommittee hear from professionals representing an area
of the public school curriculum not consulted on the initial commission report.

The disciplines represented by the American Alliance teach both the
physical skills and the cognitive knowledge necessary for a healthy
and productive life. These disciplines represent a discrete body of
knowledge essential to the development of our nation's youth. If

placed on the agenda, we intend to present testimony to the committee along the following lines:

- The Commission's report waves the national defense banner to justify more and better science and math courses. Meanwhile, the Department of Defense is establishing remedial physical education programs because new inductees do not possess the physical skills necessary to defend our country. Health and physical education are important to our nation's defense.

- The Commission's report maintains that our country is falling behind foreign interests in business and industry. And yet, many forward-thinking foreign competitors (as well as successful American companies) have risen to the top of their industry with a new emphasis on the health and fitness of the employee. Health and physical education are vital to our nation's businesses and economy.

- The rising costs of health care are draining our personal and public pocketbooks. Preventive health education can make substantial gains in slashing the cost of illness. Health and physical education is important to the health of our country's domestic budget.

- Heart disease continues to be the number one American killer. Physical fitness, exercise, proper nutrition and a healthy lifestyle can prevent and minimize the effects of cardiovascular disease. Health and physical education are important to our citizens' health and longevity.

- Drunk driving has become a serious problem for all Americans, but particularly for our nation's youth. Drug abuse and alcoholism threaten to cripple our children's health and their future. Nancy Reagan has said, "Teachers can raise the awareness of drugs and drunk driving through serious class discussions of how to reverse peer pressure." Health and physical education—where such discussions occur—may be critical to the very lives of our children.

- The 1984 Olympics which will be held in the United States can demonstrate in a very real and public way that we have what it takes to compete with the rest of the world—individually and as a nation. Health and physical education are important to our national image.

The Commission report speaks of developing the "individual powers of the mind and spirit to the utmost." But what about the body? The Olympic ideal, which still remains valid, is the triad of mind-spirit-body. How, in good conscience, can we tell our children to tend to

their minds and spirits and neglect their physical relationship to
their world?

The health behaviors established in youth become the health habits of
adulthood. Excellence in education means much more than the expansion
of science, math, and computer programs. Excellence means more than
economic competition in the market place. Excellence means giving our
youth meaningful, systematic, and professional instruction. In the
words of the Commission, excellence means "that all children by virtue
of their own efforts, competently guided, can hope to attain mature and
informed judgment needed to secure gainful employment and manage their
own lives, thereby serving not only their own interests but also the
progress of society itself." Through health and physical education,
children learn the joy of their own efforts. They learn discipline.
They learn to set goals, and to achieve them. They learn to manage
their own bodies and their lives to serve themselves and their society.
They learn the meaning of excellence.

Thank you for your consideration. I look forward to hearing from you
soon.

Sincerely,

Margaret M. Seiter
Director, Public and
    Legislative Affairs

MMS/mp

Sample: Proclamation

WHEREAS, fifty-four percent of all deaths in the United States result from diseases of the heart and blood vessels and are associated with physical inactivity;

WHEREAS, the ordinary tasks of daily living no longer provide vigorous exercise to develop and maintain cardiovascular and respiratory fitness, and most Americans do not engage in appropriate physical activity either during recreation or in the course of their work;

WHEREAS, substantial physical and emotional benefits direct and indirect are possible with regular physical fitness and exercise;

WHEREAS, inactivity in children can influence mature functional capacity and may be directly related to a number of adult health problems;

WHEREAS, physical activity is necessary to support the normal growth in children, and is essential to the continuing health and well-being of youth and adults;

WHEREAS, it is important to develop attitudes conducive to physical activity early in life, and during grades 1-6, children quickly develop physical skills and attitudes difficult to change;

WHEREAS, the 60 million school-aged children and youth have the potential to acquire the knowledge, skills, and values that can lead to a lifetime of healthful living;

THEREFORE, be it resolved that the Central State Parents and Teachers Association strongly supports physical education as integral to the curriculum for all children in grades K-12.

7

Practicalities for Lobbying Techniques

Before writing a letter, or visiting legislators or representatives, make some notes about what to say. Describe the strategic message. List three things that the person should remember afterwards. Rehearse the visit to gain more confidence. Take a look at the following information.

Letter Writing

Format

- Use standard business letter format.
- Use plain white typing paper (8 1/2 x 11 inches). Use stationery with letterhead if the letter is from the association.
- Type the letter
- Use a black typewriter ribbon and black or dark blue ink for the signature.
- Include the date of the letter, a complete mailing address, name, and telephone number.
- Sign the letter. Anonymous letters carry no weight.
- If writing to a legislator other than a local one, send a copy of the correspondence to the local legislator, indicating clearly that this has been done (cc: The Honorable Jane Jones). This is an appreciated courtesy.
- Address legislators properly. (Figure 7.1).

Writing Tips

- Be clear, concise, and courteous.
- Avoid abusive or threatening language.
- Get to the point. Describe the reason for writing the letter in the first sentence or paragraph. Don't give the entire history of recreation and parks.
- Check grammar and word usage. Do not be afraid to ask friends for help.
- Do not use a large word when a small one does the job.
- Use strong verbs and the active voice.
- Make language specific. Use concrete words and images.
- Make the written word sound spoken.
- As a guideline, use no sentence longer than 15 words, no paragraph longer than five sentences, and no letter longer than two pages.
- Be prepared to make at least three drafts. Use the first to get some ideas down on paper, the second to clarify and order ideas persuasively, and the last to refine the letter's style and tone.

Address Your Legislators Properly!

Addressee	Form of Address	Salutation
Local		
Alderman	The Honorable John Smith	Dear Mr. Smith
Commissioner	The Honorable John Smith	Dear Mr. Smith
Mayor	The Honorable John Smith Mayor of _____	Dear Mayor Smith
State		
State Representative*	The Honorable John Smith House of Representatives State Capitol	Dear Mr. Smith
Governor	The Honorable John Smith Governor of _____ State Capitol Anywhere, USA	Dear Governor Smith
State Senator	The Honorable John Smith State Senate State Capitol	Dear Senator Smith
National		
U.S. Representative*	The Honorable John Smith The United States House of Representatives Washington, D.C. 20515	Dear Mr. Smith
U.S. Senator	The Honorable John Smith The United States Senate Washington, D.C. 20510	Dear Senator Smith

Figure 7.1 Proper Methods of Address

Content

- Each letter should deal with only one issue so that it goes to the appropriate staffer without getting shuffled around the office.
- Be as specific as possible. Mention a bill number (if it's available). Tell what action is desired. Leave the legislator in no doubt as to which way to vote.
- Back up opinion with a calmly reasoned argument and hard facts. Do not forget that the goal is to convince, not offend.
- Tell a legislator why he or she should be concerned. If possible, establish a connection between the home district and the issue. Explain what repercussions might occur in a district.
- Always state the organization's name clearly.

- Describe the organization in terms of number of members, the number of people members can reach (annually, monthly, or in their careers), or some other figure which can let a legislator know the breadth of an organization's power base.
- Ask for a specific action in the first or last paragraph of the letter. Ask a question which will elicit an answer, such as, "How do you plan to vote on this issue?"
- Describe what the proposed legislation will mean to the organization, agency, and community. Personalize the letter.
- Let a sense of commitment show, but remain professional and reasonable.
- Write a letter as an individual. Then get local and state professional organizations and civic associations to write letters as well. The effect of one influential individual activating an extensive network of friends and colleagues can change a legislator's mind.
- If there is no response within 3 weeks, write a follow-up letter. If there is a crucial vote approaching, make a follow-up phone call.
- Be constructive. If the major intent of the bill is good, but there are possible operational problems, offer solutions which would be more effective and workable. Legislators cannot be experts in every area.
- Do not pretend to wield vast political influence. Do not profess to be a self-appointed spokesperson for an association or profession. Such a claim will leave credibility in doubt, and lessen the chance that views will be taken seriously.
- Do not become a legislative pen pal. Writing to a legislator on every issue, or answering every response with another letter will also lessen credibility.
- Support the legislators. Often people write letters only to tell politicians what they are doing wrong. Be sure to write in support of a bill or issue which local legislators favor.

Visiting a Representative

A personal visit is an effective way to communicate with representatives. Meet the legislators in their home offices. Being there makes an impact that paper cannot. A face to face meeting provides an opportunity not only to speak personally about concerns, but also to begin a long-term relationship. The following suggestions will help make the most of a visit.

Getting Ready

Make an appointment as far ahead of time as possible. Chances of meeting with a representative (rather than a staffer) increase. State the case directly. Appointment or no, it is possible to meet with an aide instead of a representative. This can be an advantage. An aide may be more knowledgeable about a particular issue and may have more time to talk about it. Legislators depend on the opinions and advice of their staff.
- Prepare a fact sheet on an issue to give the legislator or aide afterwards.
- Prepare mentally. Be very clear about purpose. Plan to stick to one subject. Know what actions the representative should take. Ask how he or she plans to vote.
- Review the representative's record. Be prepared to refer to particular actions, such as votes or public statements, that relate to the issue in question.
- If the visit relates to a particular bill, refer to it by name and number. Know who introduced it and what it proposes.
- Be able to discuss the bill's impact on the legislator's home district.
- Be ready to give reasons for a particular position on an issue. Representatives are interested in personal experiences and observations.
- Dress neatly in appropriate business attire.

In the Office

- Take advantage of the waiting time to ask the secretary how the mail is running for and against the issue in question.
- When meeting the representative, after introductions, tell him or her whether an organization has sponsored the visit. Mention residence in his or her district. Mention personal occupation, involvement in community affairs, and (as a member of his or her party) activities with the political party and the most recent campaign. Mention any mutual friends or acquaintances.
- State concerns, and inquire about the legislator's familiarity with the issue. Find out where he or she stands, and try to figure out which of several planned arguments would be most effective. The goal is to educate, communicate and persuade.
- If the asks a question, get an answer and follow up immediately.
- If you feel the legislator is intentionally or unintentionally changing the topic, steer the conversation back to it. Recognize as dodges such general comments as "You've presented some interesting ideas," or "I'll certainly take your views into consideration."
- State point of view clearly and back it up with reasoned arguments. Don't be argumentative.
- Show familiarity with the legislator's record, especially any part of it relative to the issue.

Leaving

- Thank the representative for his or her time.
- Present a fact sheet on the issue.
- Ask to be placed on mailing lists.
- Sign the guest book, if one is available.

Follow-Up

As soon as possible, make notes on key points of the conversation.
- Always write a thank you letter. Whether or not the legislator has voted the "right" way, t hank him or her for listening. Remain courteous, and remind him or her that constituent's will still be watching during the next vote and the next election.

Hearings

When preparing for a public hearing, find answers to the following questions.
- Know the time limit for testimony, whether is is 3 minutes or 20 minutes.
- Find out if the committee is trying to get a range of opinions from all key organizations.
- Know how big the committee room is.
- Discover how many observers are expected.
- Know the speaking schedule, the layout of the building, and whether parking is available.
- Find out when to arrive.
- Be prepared for press coverage.

Tips for Public Hearings

- All testimony should be typed, double spaced, and photocopied (not mimeographed).
- Bring copies for all committee members plus extras for the press and other participants.
- Bring background pieces as well.
- Advise the press that the speech will take place. Follow up with phone calls and a press release.
- It is possible to hold pre-testimony press luncheons.
- Make testimony lively, clear, and persuasive.
- Do not list all the things the committee did wrong. Do not chastise them. Persuade them. List the reasons why it is imperative that they include recreation and parks issues. A public hearing provides a unique opportunity to sell ideas.

8

Tools for the Media

Understand the rules of the game. Establish a plan of action. There are some tools that will help communicate, educate, and influence public policy decision makers.

Public Relations

Communicate with the media is communication with the public. The media is a conduit to and ultimately a multiplier of influence. Legislators are also part of the public and are influenced by the media. One article or TV news story reaches many more citizens than personal contacts. Good communication means having a general understanding of how people listen, what makes news, and the issues that need to be communicated.

Image

What people think about an association, recreation and parks, and government in general is important to credibility. A speaker must be credible before communication can occur. Public perception of issues and organizations plays an important part in how legislators perceive and listen to any argument.

Many businesses and industries have public relations firms and advertising agencies that function as professional media communicators. Such professionals have the luxury of money and the mandate to build an image for their company over time. Without the luxury, association's goals are the same.

Consider the example of a brokerage firm, with a target audience of males over 50 with $100,000 or more in income. Their goal is to convey an image of trust, integrity, security, and stability. They might choose an older white male as their spokesperson--someone who evokes trust--a Walter Cronkite type. They might use full page ads in *Fortune* and the *Wall Street Journal*. Their spokesperson, message, and vehicles for their message would be entirely different from that of a soft drink company.

By contrast, the soft drink company wants to appeal to a 15-30 year-old age group which is racially and sexually mixed, middle class, and active. They may use television ads with beach scenes, surfing, swimming, and volleyball to sell their product. Rather than one spokesperson, they would use a young, active group. Their image is youth, activity, and their drink equal good times! The ingredients, message, vehicle, spokesperson, script, and scenery-in each presentation are carefully chosen to convey both the message and a more subtle image of the product and the company.

Learn From Images

Learn form the experts. Associations might not be able to afford high priced public relations firms, but they can teach by example. Decide on the public image an organization means to convey.List key words that describe the association, such as professional, active, accessible, reasonable, supportive, and a friend to children. Mention association programs that supporter families and the community An image can be positive or negative. Define the organization's image and communicate that image effectively. Show how supporting recreation and parks issues can make a community more liveable for its members. Do not communicate internal differences of opinion to the public. Do not communicate professional disagreements. Communicate an image that helps the public identify positively with the organization. A positive image is consistency. Every member who speaks, writes, or testifies should be aware of the image that the organization wants to convey. Clearly communicate goals to members. The tone and substance of the message, the vehicle, the spokesperson, and the representatives should reflect those goals.

Another key to successful communication is repetition. There are thousands of messages being thrown at everyone everyday, from television, radio, newspapers, magazines, and professional journals, from friends and colleagues, from our families, and from our children. There is more information available than can be taken in. Messages of importance must be filtered out, and assigned importance. Each message is just one of many. Repetition increases the chance any message has of being heard.

Strategic Messages

To communicate a message well, be consistent and repetitive. A message that communicates is simple, straightforward, and easy to understand. It should be expressed in clear, simple sentences.

"Public recreation and parks facilities need your support if they are to serve you best."

"Recreation and parks activities improve the quality of life of your citizens in your community and state."

"Recreation and parks activities teach good citizenship."

Choose a Vehicle

A communication vehicle is a method used to carry a message to the public, such as a letter, press release, television interview show, or magazine article. Although many vehicles communicate to the public, it is difficult to choose the vehicle that will communicate quickly, clearly and effectively to any target audience. in matching communications vehicles to an audience, consider the following:

- Reach a target audience.
- The vehicle should expose the message to target groups.
- Get the most exposure for time and money spent.
- Use resources most effectively, with least risk of backlash or bad public image.
- Time the message to be most effective.

In short, a good communication vehicle serves because it is on target, effective, economical, and timely.

What is News

New is information that has not been reported before. Just as the name implies, it is new. The value of news is determined by the impact a piece of information has on a large segment of the public. Certain subjects generally get good coverage, but all are subject to the particular "window of interest" the public attributes to them. Drunk driving, which got little play before the inception of groups like MADD (mothers Against Drunk Driving), suddenly received front page coverage because ordinary people got involved in what was formerly perceived as a bureaucratic issue. Although state safety agencies have spent millions of dollars on drunk driving public information programs for more than 20 years, the news now is that hundreds of people are organizing campaigns to solve a social problem.

It is possible to use this example to good advantage. Fitness is one of today's most popular issues. Millions of runners, skaters, climbers, swimmers, and bicyclists are involved in fitness programs. Any issue that affects many people is news. Remember that recreation and parks activities and facilities provide unique opportunities for members of the community to become fit.

News:
- is new
- interests many people
- affects many people

News Moves Fast. Yesterday's news is not news anymore. Issues change quickly. By the time an important issue surfaces, it may be too late to organize a position. Make contacts before an issue breaks. Establish a reputation for fairness, openness and intelligence. Be ready to respond when an issue heats up.

Hard News/Feature News

Members of the press generally try to divide hard news from feature news. Hard news stories concern political elections, crime, and legislative decisions. Feature news centers on the human element, on human interest. Feature news can convey information that is interesting or "newsy." Feature news is more durable, and therefore takes a back seat to more "perishable" hard news.

News Peg

When trying to capture a reporter's attention, establish the fact that the issue currently interests the public. Reporters call this a news peg. A news peg is the element of a story that relates to a current event. Without it, the news story is irrelevant. News pegs are the hooks on which a reporter hangs a story. When trying to discuss an issue with a reporter, establish the news peg quickly. The reporter can use it to see and to convey to readers the relevance of an issue.

Dealing With the Media

When dealing with the news media, keep two things in mind. First, remember the goal. Decide on a strategic message. Communicate the message. Second, understand the position of the readers or public receiving the message. Each reporter has a frame of reference. Market an idea. To be effective, give the reporter what he wants (and what the organization wants).

Newspaper editors choose one story over another every day. The relationship between effective behavior change in members of a physical education class and class size may be a great story, but it may not be an editor's choice. Give an editor a reason to make space to this story. Know what editors are they looking for. Give them what they need. Make their job easier, so they'll call next time they need a quote.

How to Deal with a Reporter

A reporter's job is collecting and simplifying information. Help a reporter do that job, and make a friend. Hinder the reporter, and make a foe. Here are some rules to follow in dealing with reporters.
- Don't play favorites, but cultivate friendly reporters who are interested in recreation and parks issues. Take advantage of their interest.
- Never speak off the record.
- Be friendly, but remain professional.
- Recognize that the reporter's time is valuable. Use it wisely.
- Always ask if there is something else the reporter needs. Giving a reporter additional information is a good way to maintain continued contact.
- Develop a reputation as a news source so the reporter will call when he needs a quotable response to an event.
- Don't be shy about talking to reporters; they can absorb quantities of information. Remember the difference between a published or unpublished story may be the preparedness of the first person the reporter thinks to contact. Know the facts and be prepared to discuss them.

Accuracy in Reporting

Accurate reporting is an issue as old as the first newspaper. Reporters gather facts quickly, work on short deadlines, and often are hampered by time, circumstances, or people, from getting all sides of an issue. No one likes inaccuracy. The overwhelming majority of reporters and editors try hard to get the story straight. Help them.

- Talk to reporters face-to-face, if possible. The telephone doesn't communicate facial expression or show documents, photographs or other pertinent evidence.
- Have an open policy with reporters that shows eagerness to make full disclosure of organization activities.
- Reduce issues to simple terms. Make them simple and easy to understand. Reporters want to write stories for the average intelligent reader. Help them get the details, issues, and facts straight.
- Repeat major strategic messages. The agenda should be to communicate issues to the public. Restating major points helps reporters understand the organization's perspective, and how it differs from other points of view.
- Give the reporter written material. Highlight key statements. Give reporters names, addresses, titles, even telephone numbers of key players. Do not deal in acronyms--they are insiders' codes. Neither the public, nor the reporter should be expected to understand an organization's acronyms.
- Do not ask to see the story before it goes to print. No reporter will allow that. A good reporter may call back to confirm the conversation.
- Note misquotes. Call the reporter. Call the editor. Ask for a correction if the misquote was serious. Otherwise merely express disappointment, and ask for ways to ensure fair coverage in the future (Editors may not know reporters are inaccurate unless they are told.).

Techniques for Media Attention

Several standard vehicles communicate with the press. To develop a good relationship with reporters, think of ways in which to help them do their job and get a good story quickly.

News Release

A news release is the most common way to communicate a complex issue or message to the public via the media. Designed to give reporters accurate information on a news event or issue, a release may announce an upcoming event, record an event, or convey facts surrounding an issue. It should convey information quickly in an easy-to-use form. Normally written in newspaper style, the form should allow an editor with a tight deadline to edit and typeset the piece quickly. The purpose is to make it easy for the reporter to use the information for a news story (See Practicalities at the end of this section.).

A news release could be written on a local recreation and park professional who has received the state recreation and park professional of the year award, or an upcoming recreation and park days event. Use the event to make the public aware of the importance of recreation and parks as part of the quality of life of the community and state. Relate the news release to an issue currently in the public mind, such as the report on Excellence in Government, and establish a news peg to get a reporter's attention.

Backgrounder

A backgrounder is usually a separate release used to provide reporters with more in-depth information, history, or background. It can also be used independently to educate a reporter on an association's position on a number of issues. Backgrounders usually define the issue, detail the reasons for its timeliness, and give the organization's views or position, often through direct quotations from leaders, skillfully worked into the body of piece. It helps the reporter deal with an issue more intelligently.

A backgrounder is especially good for complex issues. For instance, if an agency is considering a bond election for new pools, give a reporter a background piece on the history of pools, their construction, original cost, projected life span, number of annual users, number of youth who learned to swim in them, etc. The backgrounder would expose the reporter to a more thorough understanding of the larger issues.

Public Letters

Public letters communicate a position on an issue or on a policy. Often, these take the form of open letters to a board or commission. They are useful to reporters as sources of quotes and story details. The American Association for Leisure and Recreation might write an open letter to the President's Commission on Americans Outdoors to comment on the commission's recommendations. An ad hoc coalition of past Secretaries of State could write an open letter to the President of the United States on the deployment of nuclear missiles. Although the letter is sent to the organization or person to whom it is addressed, its purpose is usually quite different from a private letter. It conveys information designed to convince the public, and it is written expressly for publication. Along with the public letter, a news release could call attention to the letter and some of its key points. Public letters can find many platforms. They can be published on the editorial page, used as the basis of a news story, published in purchased advertisements.

Press Advisory

A fourth technique in using the media to communicate with the public is a press advisory. A press advisory announces the time, date, and details of an event to the press. A press advisory is often used to announce a press conference. Reporters who attend the news conference might receive additional materials: a backgrounder, news release, or press kit. The press advisory teases. Its purpose is to entice attendance. It can herald ground breaking ceremonies, fund raising events, or scheduled testimony before the state legislature.

Letter to the Editor

Another effective device to get your issue before the public is a letter to the editor. Letters to the editor are surprisingly well-read and can often provoke public awareness and debate on a previously little publicized issue. Letters to the editor should take a definite stand on an issue without being over-zealous. Accusations and personal attacks hurt the case, and are rarely published. The letter should be brief, professional, well-written, without professional jargon. The letter should relate in some way to an article, editorial, or another recently published letter to the editor. Several members may respond, or one member may respond to a letter from another member. Such a running dialogue can keep an issue before the public for days, even weeks. Letter writers and letter signers need not be the same person. A letter signed by an important community leader, a state association president, or a state legislator can be most effective. Request a letter from the national office. Individual situations need to be evaluated individually. Define the strategic message. Decide who can best speak to it. Go back to the plan.

Sidebar

Editors often use a sidebar on important stories. A sidebar is a news story which gives the local angle or a personal, human-interest approach to a larger story.

When the Department of Defense announced the closing of 91 military installations they identified potential types of uses for the facilities. A good sidebar about how other communities with base closings have utilized them for recreation and parks facilities would have been effective at that time.

Sidebars can also be keyed directly to a state or local issue. Proposed funding cutbacks in recreation and parks programs could be countered with a lively story in a high quality local program. What one therapeutic recreation leader is doing every day to contribute to handicapped students' development could accompany a story on the Special Olympics.

Opinion/Editorial Page

Opinion/editorial columns appear on the opinion and editorial page of the newspaper. These are opinion pieces, and their goal is to express a persuasive point of view. Professional newspaper columnists who appear regularly occasionally print guest columns written by people who are not professional columnists. The guest column, or opinion/editorial piece, allows a member of the public to share an opinion. Timeliness and expertise are critical. An opinion/editorial piece on the importance of recreation and parks issues as positive contributors to a community's quality of life could be used as a response to local pressure to cut support for recreation and parks. More thought provoking than newsy, an opinion/editorial piece should relate to a topic currently getting media attention.

Press Examples

Any of the following situations might arise in the course of taking action. These are examples, not formulas; they are illustrative, not prescriptive. Each situation warrants a creative approach and individual solution.

Situation: The state association president will testify before a state task force on opportunities to increase travel and tourism at the local level. The press should be there to report on the testimony and to make the public aware of the value of recreation and parks.

Action : Issue a press advisory to notify the media of the testimony. Write a news release to highlighting key points in the president's remarks, and a backgrounder to explain the issue. Make complete copies of the testimony available to reporters at the hearing.

Situation: The city council votes next Wednesday on whether or not to eliminate recreation and parks center leaders in a budget cutting move. Many members testified as the budget process progressed, but the vote will be close. No one is sure who will win. There will be a large turnout, and a final gesture might sway the vote to the right side.

Action: Buy a half page ad in the local paper and publish an open letter to the city council. Have community leaders sign it. It should speak to the importance of the upcoming vote to the future quality of life of your community. Simultaneously, issue a news release that summarizes the points in the ad and tells why community leaders wanted to sign on—in their own words.

Situation: A national commission just released a study on the status of recreation and parks in the United States. The report says that funding should come from all levels of government if recreation and parks are to be accessible to all. You know that the city council is about to embark on a year-long study of essential city services. Several council members already advocate reducing funding for recreation and parks issues. Move rapidly to block any further consideration of this position.

Action: Find a sympathetic reporter, and start putting backgrounders in the mail. Set up luncheon meetings with reporters. Send an open letter to the commission, and publish it in your local newspapers. Organize a speakers' bureau. Obtain speaking engagements before groups to which council members belong. Distribute literature to recreation program participants and park users showing them how they can get involved, and how to contact their local councilman.

Situation: Members are joining with local service clubs, YMCAs and YWCAs to sponsor a leisure fair at the three area shopping centers. The fairs will be held during national recreation and parks week. Alert the public and encourage attendance.

Action: Work with the newspaper to get a special feature on the style section front page. Better yet, develop a personality piece on one of the unique participants. Get a headliner to participate in the fair, perhaps as an emcee.

Be creative. These aren't rules. They are suggestions to stimulate imagination. An original approach that meets stated objectives generally gets better results.

Sample: Press Release

American Alliance

for health,
physical education,
recreation
and dance

est. 1885

1900 Association Drive Reston, Virginia (703) 476-3400

For Further Information:
Peggy Seiter, Director
Public & Legislative Affairs
(703) 476-3455

FOR IMMEDIATE RELEASE

CAHPERD President speaks at
Task Force Hearing

SACRAMENTO, CA., March 24--Removing required physical education
in elementary schools will have disastrous effects on our children's
health and wellbeing, the California Association for Health, Physical
Education, Recreation and Dance told a state Department of Education
Task Force today.

CAHPERD's President Tillman, Dean of Arts and Sciences at
Sacremento State University, called on the task force to reverse its
proposal to limit physical education for elementary school children.
The Department wants to remove an existing rule requiring students to
participate in a minimum of 20 minutes of daily physical education
instruction. The rule would be replaced by one requiring 20 minutes
of physical education only three times a week, and 20-minute "play"
or "recess" periods, twice a week.

(more)   3/24/83

CAHPERD President speaks at
Task Force Hearing

"What is happening here today, is that you are making a choice between bridges, roads, and sewers, and the education of our children," Tillman told the task force on curriculum requirements. "Given that choice, the people of California will choose education," he said.

"We believe that the California Department of Education is sacrificing the health and future of our children for one small budget cut today," said Tillman. "Although the department cites reducing educational costs as the reason for eliminating the daily requirements, they have produced no figures which show how much money would be saved by denying children this essential instruction."

"Recess is not enough!" President Tillman told the task force. "Studies have shown that left to their own devices, children seldom reach high enough levels of intensity to bring about the desired health benefits of a good physical education program. It is important that children learn early in their lives the skills, behaviors and positive self-concepts necessary to make them healthier, happier, and more productive citizens," said Tillman.

"Routine, vigorous physical activity," said Tillman, "has been shown to reduce the incidence of:

- obesity
- coronary disease
- hypertension

- diabetes
- musculoskeletal problems and
- depression anxiety."

(more)   3/24/83

CAHPERD President speaks at
Task Force Hearing

"Grades 1 through 6 is the ideal time for children to develop basic motor skills. At this age, children quickly learn physical skills which they can build on at a later time in their life," said Tillman. "Research has shown that attitudes are developed at a young age, and once formed, are difficult to change."

Tillman offered to provide additional information on the short and long term benefits of physical education to the task force.

The state board of education has appointed the task force to gather input from the public concerning changes in curriculum. A CAHPERD representative has testified at each of the hearings, which have been taking place around the state for the past six months.

-30-

Sample: Letter to the Editor

Letters

Teacher termination bill questioned

To the Editor of The Tribune:

The Iowa Association for Health, Physical Education, Recreation and Dance has not taken a stand on the Teacher Termination Bill (Senate File 448) but would like to voice its concern with Section 280.13 of the bill which pertains to the separation of teaching and coaching duties. The proposed bill greatly decreases the requirements for coaching athletic teams. Whereas at this time a coach is required to have a teacher's certificate and to have a coaching endorsement the current bill does away with the requirement for the teaching certificate. Rather, it stipulates that the only requirement for coaching would be to have a coaching endorsement. The coaching requirements are not standardized and currently can be satisfied by taking abbreviated courses on two weekends. These courses do not have the same amount of content as those currently taught in the universities. Under the proposed legislation anyone, even a high school dropout who took a couple of weekend courses, could spend two or three hours a day coaching students in a sport.

Our major concerns center around these issues:

1) This legislation represents a major philosophic change regarding the place of sports in the schools. While heretofore, sports have been considered part of the overall instructional program of the school, the implication of S.F. 448, Section 280.13 is that athletics are not part of the educational setting and are outside instructional guidelines. A coach who is not part of the educational system would not have the informal day to day contact in the schools such as those that take place in the hallway, the classroom, and the times before and after practice to talk with the student athlete. Those contacts are important and allow a teacher coach to show a concern for the student's total development and school life.

2) Coaching requires a knowledge of physiological processes, an understanding of developmental psychology, and acquaintance with educational techniques. Such things as warm-up process, training regimens, work-out plans, and expectations at certain levels comprise an integral part of coaching preparation and a coach without formal preparation in these areas would be shortchanging students. The possibility of injury in sport would be greater conceivably resulting in more legal suits against the school.

Our neighbor state, Minnesota, currently has separate contracts for teaching and coaching but the requirements for coaching certification are almost the equivalent for those teaching physical education. We feel we owe it to Iowa students to provide the best we have to offer and that this section of the proposed bill diminishes those opportunities.

Jan Beran
IAHPERD President
311 Physical Education Building
Ames, Iowa

Wayne Osness

Alliance President Responds to Commission

On April 26th, the White House released a report from the National Commission on Excellence in Education entitled "A Nation at Risk: The Imperative for Educational Reform." The report sounds a warning to educators across the nation: We have let our educational system decline; the results have affected our economy, our industries, our children, and the safety and security of our nation and our future. The message is clear: America cannot afford to continue to tolerate the status quo in education.

The Commission report made public many issues and concerns that educators have been sharing with each other for some time now. From American Alliance members we have often heard: "Some of our majors come to us neither with the rudimentary essentials in math and science, nor the physical skills needed to continue their learning at the college level." "Students seem interested only in getting by, getting the credentials necessary to get a job."

One can argue selected points of the commission's findings, the logic and practicality of their recommendations, or the dirge-like seriousness of their warnings. But what cannot be argued is that this report is long overdue and is very likely to signal a renaissance in education which will precipitate major changes in the very fabric of our educational system—the impact will reach far into the future. We may be on a critical threshold. The possibilities are infinite and exciting.

But there are also some ominous implications. One of the major criticisms the commission levies at the current system is that "Twenty-five percent of the credits earned by general-track high school students are in physical education and health education, work experience outside the school, remedial English and mathematics, and personal service and development courses, such as training for adulthood and marriage . . ."

The commission believes that these courses take time away from math, science, English and social studies courses, thereby contributing to the decline in the overall level of educational achievement of our nation's students.

The American Alliance disagrees with this inference on two counts. First, grouping physical education and health education courses with remedial courses, training for adulthood and experiences which occur outside the school denigrates our professions, which *are* part of the educational mainstream. The teaching skills, knowledge, and appreciation of movement is an essential part of a complete, well-rounded education. Developing an understanding and awareness of an active lifestyle on an individual and personal level is an integral part of the school curriculum of the future.

Second, the implication that somehow these courses have contributed to a diminished educational performance could not be further from the truth.

Physical education and health education classes are not the cause of the declining level of student achievement; they can and do serve as an impetus for higher achievement. Physical education teaches skills and knowledge which can be used throughout a student's lifetime, resulting in a healthier, more physically fit adult. Increased levels of physical activity bring increased capacity for productivity. A physically active person is a more productive person. A physically active person is tired less often and finds an increased level of energy. Physically active and fit students, therefore, will have more, not less time and energy.

Physical education and health education teach students about healthy diet, good nutrition and how their bodies function. Students who eat right and engage in regular physical activity will be healthier and will be absent from school less often. Students who are knowledgeable about their bodies and who are in good physical condition use less energy to accomplish goals, and maintain an efficiency of movement which can leave more time for learning.

Physical education teaches students how to use their leisure time. Appropriate use of leisure time provides a much needed respite to the rigors of a demanding new educational curriculum, allowing better concentration and increased attention span while on task.

Health education teaches students about the care and maintenance of

9

Practicalities for Using Tools for the Media

Press Release Format

When writing a press release, remember the six questions that the release should answer: who, what, where, when, why and how. Always put the most important information first and the least important last. Omit anything not pertinent to the issue. Check writing tips in the following section.

Use the standard format for writing a news release.

- Use standard 8 1/2" x 11" white paper and black typewriter ribbon. Colored paper might draw attention to a newsletter, but it will look unprofessional in a news release.
- The release should be typewritten, and printed or photocopied. The quality of mimeographed releases is inadequate.
- Use one side of the paper only.
- Use wide margins. Double space. Use association letterhead or special news release stationery, which includes the organization's name, address, and phone number.
- Label the first page clearly as a news release.
- Give the name and title of a contact person and that person's day and evening phone numbers in the upper left hand corner of every page. Type "For Immediate Release" prominently near the top of the first page. If it should be released on a particular day, type, "For Release: May 16, 19__, after 10 a.m."
- Do not let a sentence or paragraph carry over from one page to the next.
- Do not hyphenate words.
- A news release should rarely be more than two pages long. At the top left hand side of the second and subsequent pages , list the name of the organization and the page number, i.e. "American Alliance, Page 2."
- If the release is more than one page, type "(MORE)" at the bottom of all but the final page. On the last page indicate the end of the release by the symbol "-30- "or "###."

Writing Tips

- Be clear, concise, and courteous.
- Get to the point.
- Use a news peg.
- Write "inverted pyramid style," most important information first, and then add details.
- Check grammar and word usage. Do not be afraid to ask friends for help.
- Do not use a big word when you can a small one is as or more effective.

- Use strong verbs. Write in the active voice.
- Quote several key sources, if appropriate. Quote accurately.
- Be specific.
- Make your writing style natural, reflecting conversational tone.
- Use concrete words and images.
- Use this guideline: No sentences should be longer than 15 words, no paragraph longer than five sentences, and no press release longer than two pages.
- Be prepared to make at least three drafts: the first to get some ideas down on paper, the second to clarify and order the ideas, and the last to refine the press release style and tone.

Dealing With Printers

If a large number of releases must be mailed, they could be printed. The general rule is that it is cheaper to print (off-set) more than 100 copies, than to photocopy them. Use a quick-print printer. Their rates are usually cheaper because they use a printing process which involves a less expensive printing plate.

Printers often have machines which can collate, fold, and stuff news releases. A printer can print the news release on letterhead or news release stationery, and should offer advice about other details of the job. Don't be intimidated by big machines and unfamiliar terms. Simply ask the printer to explain details, such as paper stock, size reduction, bleed-offs, and so on.

Developing a Mailing List

Several groups of people, in addition to local newspaper editors, should be included on a mailing lists for regular press releases. This may be a good way to keep certain people up to date on an issue. Recipients of releases are chosen based on decisions made after considering the organization's legislative goals, strategic message, target audience, and the effect of the legislative struggle on the organization's image. Consider the plan. Be sure to assign someone to keep the mailing list updated.

Do not use names for media mailings. Address the envelope to "City Desk," "State Desk," "Sports Editor," or "News Editor." Editors do not mind this and it keeps the list from becoming outdated. Consider the following when developing a mailing list.

Print Media
- Local, daily, or weekly newspapers (often large cities have suburban newspapers in addition to the larger daily paper)
- Neighborhood newspapers
- Shoppers newspapers or supplements
- Newspaper supplements, i.e. special annual section on education or fitness
- State capitol newspaper (usually one newspaper in the state capitol carries state wide news)
- Minority or ethnic group newspapers
- Underground press
- Community magazines
- Special audience newspapers or newsletters
- State magazines (i.e., Texas)
- City magazines (i.e., Washington, Los Angeles)
- Regular or feature columnists, or editorial page editors.
- Trade press editors
     state recreation and park newsletters and magazines
     local department newsletters
     newsletters for local/state fitness clubs, recreation clubs, runners' clubs, YMCAs, YWCAs, Boy Scouts, etc.
     Journal of Physical Education, Recreation, and Dance
     Update

Parks and Recreation
Dateline: NRPA
Association magazines/newsletters
Regional/District Professional magazines/newsletters

Broadcast Media

- Local television stations
- Local cable television stations
- Local radio stations (check pop, rock, country, classical, all news, ethnic, urban contemporary--everyone votes and needs to know)
- Television and radio editorial and editorial response spots
- Television and radio talk show host

Community Group Newsletters

See Community Resources listing in Research and Resources Section.

Government Officials

- State boards of education members
- Governor
- State director of natural resources department
- State superintendent of schools
- State administrator of parks division
- State board of health
- State drug abuse board
- State traffic safety board
- State advisory boards
- State legislators
- State legislative chairs of education, appropriations committees
- State curriculum planning committees
- United States senators and congressmen
- Governor's Council on Physical Fitness and Sports

10

Want More?

Although the preceding information probably covers almost any situation, occasionally, additional efforts may be needed in a close legislative campaign. Additional vehicles generally require more time, money, and sophistication, so do not be afraid to ask for help. Recognize the value of using a professional in the field. They will probably be glad to offer their opinions and guidance.

Press Kits

A press kit is a collection of informational material about a particular issue, packaged in an attractive and usable form for a reporter. Press kits can contain a variety of information and usually come in a two pocket folder format. More expensive folders are printed with the issue, date, organization, and logo on the outside. Press kits can be mailed to reporters, but are most often given away at press conferences. Press kits are more visually appealing, elaborate and expensive communications vehicles than simple information. Do not use them inappropriately. Use them for impact. Use a press kit for major legislative campaigns.

- Take the offensive. Persuade a legislator to introduce a bill which would create a Council on recreation and parks.
- Initiate an annual legislative leisure day which will test state legislators' personal leisure ethics and practices, educate them about the components of good leisure, and the professional training necessary to become a recreation and park professional.

Press kits can contain a variety of information, based on the issue, the strategy, and the target audience. Some of the possible items to include in a press kit about a new piece of draft legislation might be:

- A news release announcing the introduction of the bill and explaining its significance.
- A fact sheet explaining the major points of the legislation and why it is necessary. Explain the organization's standpoint, rather than the opposition's.
- A list of people to call for more information.
- Past news releases from related activities, such as a release covering the way Illinois successfully does the same thing that this bill suggests. Show the local angle by explaining how the bill will affect student at a nearby school.
- A copy of the draft legislation.
- A short biography of the sponsor to give him credit for introducing the bill and to give him or her an opportunity for some news coverage.
- A list of cosponsors.
- Charts and graphs of data which support the cause.
- Questions and answers on key ways in which the bill is new or different. Make them questions a reporter might ask.
- A brochure of about the state organization. Do not overdo this information unless the press kit focuses on the organization.
- A list of supporters, including letters of support from other legislators and civic groups. This defines the bill's support, and lets the media know how broad-based the support is, that it is truly a community issue.

- Use good judgement about other items to be included. The goal is to educate the reporter as quickly as possible, and to provide proper background information without overburdening.

News Conferences

A news conference enables a news source to assemble a large number of reporters from a variety of media, and disseminate information to all of them at once. Press conferences are only used for major announcements. If used frivolously or inappropriately, they can harm an organization's reputation.

Press conferences take a great deal of planning and coordination. If a press conference would give the legislative campaign an extra boost, solicit the help of a public relations professional. Try to find a public relations professional who is willing to volunteer for the association. Local college or university public relations staff might be good choices. Try to get help from the public relations staff of the bill's sponsor.

Broadcast Coverage

Although you probably won't use television coverage is expensive and not often feasible, do not neglect its powerful impact on the public. Radio is far more accessible, although coverage is less global. There are different kinds of exposure, such as radio and television, local news shows, local interview shows, editorial replies, features, documentaries and public service announcements. In general, local news shows, editorial replies, and local interview shows work best to influence legislative issues.

Television News

Television news coverage is used for more important stories. Many local television stations have expanded local news segments which air daily before the national news. These shows developed because of earlier FCC regulations requiring a certain amount of local programming.

Local news show video taped footage shot earlier in the day for airing on evening or late telecasts. Some stations will do live interviews on the air. TV producers avoid "talking heads" by trying to get more visually appealing pictures. Think action when thinking about TV.

Radio News

Radio is an instant medium. Reporters use their two-way radios to report live from anywhere in the area. Recording tape can be edited and aired quickly, and stations air news at regular times during the hour, as well as more frequently when a story is breaking.

Thus radio has an incredible appetite for stories, new stories, stories that affect schools, stories that listeners want to hear. A stream of news releases, letters, and phone calls helps the news editor add an issue to the steady stream of ongoing news.

Interview Shows

Reaching a well-known local talk show personality is another way to generate interest in a topic. Well-timed, the interview can help sway the public and influence legislators. The spokesperson must be of intrinsic interest to get on the show, and must be very educated about the strategic message and image that needs to be conveyed.

Editorials

Editorial replies on radio or television are usually 60-second spots aired in response to a local news commentary, or relevant to some community issue. Often, stations look for groups with issues to present. Although they are directed by the FCC to allow responsible parties to reply, they are not required to do so. Because they cover a broad range of issues, they may not air an issue repeatedly. A simple phone call or letter to the station requesting editorial time, briefly explaining the reason for presenting the issue may secure air time. Be sure the reply is coherent, simple, and well timed. It must fit exactly into the time slot allowed. Type replies,double or triple spaced, and practice delivery.

Talking Tips

Here are some tips for projecting a good image on the air.
- Call to confirm the date, time, and place of the interview.
- Think of the interview as an offensive rather than a defensive activity. Communicate and persuade. Do not defend.
- Establish two or three points that the audience should take with them (the strategic messages) Work toward mentioning these early in the interview. Repeat and repeat them again.
- Role-play. Have a friend ask all the questions which could be asked on the air, and prepare concise, clear responses. Practice.
- Wear subdued colors for television,but not white. Avoid loud clothes. Everything is magnified on camera. Do not wear jangling jewelry or anything that makes a noise. The microphone will pick up the sound.
- Get to the station early.
- Relax.
- Do not assume that the audience knows issues or the profession.
- Talk in a relaxed, conversational tone.
- Find out when the editorial will be aired. Notify all appropriate names on the list. Be sure to thank the interviewer and the crew.

Press Luncheons

A press luncheon is an informal business meeting with one member of the press, or a more formal session with a dozen reporters. Individual press luncheons provide an atmosphere in which long-term personal relationships with reporters can be fostered, but should only be held when there is something important to say. Larger luncheons are good for explaining background information and presenting a news story. The setting, is the same as for a news conference, except more cordially presented.

Call a reporter for a luncheon meeting to give background on the state park funding bill pending in the House Appropriations Subcommittee. Set up a luncheon meeting to inform a reporter that the city council vote on a pertinent issue tonight (that didn't show up on the agenda) will be protested by 100 participants. Ask the reporter to plan for a photographer if there will be a good visual story.

Tips for press luncheons:
- Always be honest, accurate, reliable, and enthusiastic. Most importantly, build and maintain credibility.
- If meeting with only one reporter, let the reporter select the restaurant, but make the reservation in person. Otherwise, plan to rent a banquet room at a local restaurant or hotel.
- Prepare handouts concerning the information related to the discussion that can be taken away.
- Promise to send information requested, and do so the same day, if possible.
- Pay for lunch. Some papers have a policy preventing reporters from accepting, but make a sincere offer. This is courtesy, not bribery.
- Larger luncheons may be more formal, with charts and graphs presentations after a chatty meal. (Note: Make sure any information lives up to the reporter's investment of time.) An hour is usually the maximum time reporters can spare.

11

Research Excerpts:
Recreation and Parks Facts

The old saying, "Statistics can prove anything," is very true. In the same way, it could be said that research can prove anything. Both findings and their numerical analyses can be debated, researched, and analyzed again. It is often difficult to know when all the facts are in. That's why experiments are replicated many times before the profession accepts the "truth" of the findings.

Political process does not wait for research. Politically active professionals must act on the best information available at the time of a decision. The following section contains statements which have been culled from several sources, that are intended as suggestions to advocates for recreation and parks issues. Nothing negative about recreation and parks will be found here. It is not a definitive or balanced research piece, but a practical aid. When writing to legislators, preparing testimony, and speaking to community leaders, use these statements to formulate arguments or stimulate thinking.

The Research Excerpts are organized in the following order:
1. The Shape of America's Recreation and Park System
   - The Federal Level
   - The State and Local Level
2. The Benefits of Recreation and Parks
   - Health and Fitness
   - Social
   - Attitude
   - Productivity
3. What people say about Recreation and Parks
4. The Status of Recreation and Parks
   - Participation
   - Resources
5. Demand

1. The Shape of America's Recreation and Park System

The Federal Level

"...We found that we are facing a deterioration of the natural resource base, and of the recreation infrastructure. Accelerating development of our remaining open spaces, wetlands, shorelines, historic sites, and countrysides, and deferred maintenance and care of our existing resources, are robbing future generations of the heritage which is their birthright." (PCAO *Recommendations*, 1986, p. 6)

A Government Accounting Office report suggested the National Park Service would experience a $1.9 billion maintenance shortfall.

The State and Local Level

"City recreation areas and open spaces are essential links in our national network of outdoor resources, key components in a continuum that extends from small parks in crowded residential areas to pristine wilderness."(PCAO *Recommendations*, 1986, p.95)

In the past century, Americans have invested billions of dollars in public recreation facilities. These facilities, which are often essential to people's use and enjoyment of the outdoors, are now showing their age."(PCAO *Recommendations*, 1986, p. 169)

"A 1986 survey indicates . . . a crisis faces the state parks: 'Apart from funding what do [state] park directors see as their greatest need? For most, the highest priority is the existing system, especially fixing up neglected or obsolete facilities. . . . "(PCAO *Recommendations*, 1986, p. 170)

"All across America, people told us [President's Commission on Americans Outdoors] that recreation is a critical part of their lives. Yet our actions do not seem to reflect the premiere importance which Americans of all ages in all parts of the country attach to recreation.

• Fewer than 10% of American cities have a policy statement recognizing recreation as being necessary for the public good.

• Less than one penny of the federal dollar is spent on parks and recreation.

• Less than 1% of an estimated $80 billion given away as charitable contributions in 1986 in this country was for conservation programs."(PCAO *Recommendations*, 1986, p. 186)

"In real dollars, direct government spending for parks.and recreation has increased moderately since 1977. However, an analysis by the Conservation Foundation of state park and recreation budgets indicated that after adjustment for inflation, state spending for parks and recreation decreased 17%from 1980 to 1983. By contrast, state spending for all programs, after adjustment for inflation, fell only 0.4%."(PCAO *Recommendations*, 1986, p. 192)

"The National Recreation and Park Association estimated local parks facilities rehabilitation needs from 1981 to 1985 to be $4.26 billion."(PCAO *Recommendations*, 1986, p. 192)

"State recreation officials responding to a 1986 survey estimated their needs for federal Land and Water Conservation Fund assistance for the next 3 years at $1.7 billion. This sum was predicated on the availability of state and local matching money."(PCAO *Recommendations*, 1986, p. 192)

"Fairfax County, Virginia, reports that it will have to spend $55 million for parkland to keep up with population growth through the rest of this century."(PCAO *Recommendations*, 1986, p. 192)

"In 1985, local and state parks and recreation departments and federal land managing agencies spent $10.7 billion specifically on recreation. Most of that was for operations and facilities maintenance; smaller portions were for acquisition and facilities development and rehabilitation."(PCAO *Recommendations*, 1986, p. 193)

"While generously used--admissions have tripled since 1955--state parks are anything but generously funded. Belt tightening in state government and rapidly shrinking federal assistance have taken a heavy toll in recent years."(Gimlin, 1988)

2. The Benefits of Recreation and Parks

Health and Fitness

"Americans spent $355 billion, or about $1,500 per capita, on health care in 1983. If increased recreation participation would reduce that figure by just five percent, the national savings would amount to more than $15 billion."(PCAO *Recommendations*, 1986, p. 13)

"Recreation is very, very important for disabled individuals, not just for all the reasons that it is important for non-disabled individuals . . . but because recreation is a rehabilitation tool. We have found in our programs that individuals who become disabled often go through a real identity crisis, and they go through a period where there's a lot of self doubt, and lack of confidence. We have found that recreation gets them back on the road to recovery by increasing their self-confidence, and their strength so that they can compete in the market place. We believe this is even more important for the disabled person-than it is for the non-disabled person." (PCAO *Recommendations*, 1986, p. 13–14)

"One way to measure the health of a society is to measure the health of its citizens. Preventing the diseases of our society would, I believe, be a hopeless task without places to be alone, or places to play with our children, or places to walk with a friend." Dr. Russell Hoverman (PCAO *Recommendations*, 1986, p. 15)

"Children depend on safe available places to play. Children also need open spaces to roam and explore wild lands. The National Children and Youth Fitness Study (1984) found that physically fit children depend on services and facilities of community organizations, such as religious groups, local park and recreation departments, and private agencies."(PCAO *Recommendations*, 1986, p. 19)

"Parents, participants, and organizers recognize the value of camps and youth serving organizations as character builders for youth. A 1986 study by the University of California at Los Angeles found that teens did not use drugs if drug use conflicted with their self-images. Public and private recreation services provide opportunities for youth to feel good about themselves – to learn new skills, to gain confidence, to become winners."(PCAO *Recommendations*, 1986, p. 19)

"A frequently expressed motivation for participating in outdoor recreation is escape. This is described in a variety of ways, from 'seeking a change of pace,' to 'getting away from it all,' to 'giving the mind a rest,' to 'blowing off steam.' We are all in need of a change from the daily routine from time to time. Outdoor recreation is significant in its ability to fulfill these needs by providing a setting which is often in sharp contrast to everyday life. Those settings are often open, quiet, less demanding, and probably have a lot more natural features and fewer man-made features than our normal environment. Further, in participation, we are generally in control of the circumstances of our routine, such that we are not continually confronted with demands or needs to respond to others' wishes. We can do more for ourselves, and thus find a restoration of the sense of control over our life. It is particularly significant that this motivation is one that appears to be on the increase."(PCAO *Recommendations*, 1986, p. 13)

Social

"Outdoor recreation helps us accomplish personal goals -- fitness and longer life, family togetherness, friendship, personal reflection, and appreciation of nature and beauty. As the outdoors leads to the attainment of personal goals, it becomes a stimulant or catalyst for the achievement of the nation's social goals: health, education, employment, family cohesion, economic vitality, environmental quality."(PCAO *Recommendations*, 1986, p. 13)

"Today's fast-paced, highly technological society has produced new stresses and pressures. The home is seen as a sanctuary from stress, and travel for leisure is frequently closer to this home base. The focus on family and children has returned, causing parents to investigate and scrutinize the amenities their communities offer. Recreation programs need to be flexible, allowing participation before work, during lunch hours, or after work. Amenities, such as child care are increasingly important." (PCAO *Recommendations*, 1986, p. 24)

"Close to home recreation is important for everyone, but it is particularly critical for less mobile people who are often concentrated in the cities. Recreation helps special groups overcome social isolation. Citizens with physical and mental disabilities are often isolated from the mainstream of society by social attitudes, as well as physical and economic barriers. Recreation programs can be a first step to break down these barriers."(PCAO *Recommendations*, 1986, p. 98)

"Family groups are, by far, the most common type of group visiting public recreation areas in the United States, totalling nearly two-thirds of groups."(PCAO *Recommendations*, 1986, p. 14)

"Parkland is needed socially because a health-conscious population demands fresh air to breath and open space for running that cannot be found inside a gym."(Hornback, 1989)

"Families tend to turn to outdoor recreation activities more than to most other recreation activities when whole families participate together and group leisure is three times as likely to be done with families than with other friends and acquaintances."(West, 1986)

Attitude

"Each year thousands of nerve-shaken, overcivilized people find that going to the mountains, forest, and deserts is sort of like going home. These areas are useful not only as fountains of timber and water but fountains of life."(PCAO *Recommendations*, 1986, p. 10

"Recent studies indicate that people are staying at home more but wishing to be away at the same time. When people do get away, it is for much shorter trips than was customary before the sharp rise in travel costs after 1978."(Hornback, 1989)

"Happiness comes from facing meaningful challenges where there is a reasonable chance of success. We crave struggles where the outcome is in doubt, where there is no guaranteed success or certain failure. There may be success today and failure tomorrow but we take delight in exercising our talents." (Neal, 1983)

"Change of attitudes and firming of a philosophy come primarily through experiencing, through intense involvement in activity through which intrinsic rewards are obtained."(Neal, 1983)

"Opportunities for expression which determine the quality of youth will comely largely through one's recreation time--recreation meaning to create anew."(Neal, 1983)

"...Recreation...reaches on to creativity. Outdoor recreation demands and evokes aesthetic responses in ways for which there are no substitutes indoors. What is preserved in a park, a wilderness, a wildlife refuge, a water gap, an offshore island, a mountain on the skyline is not merely the life supporting environment; we preserve the possibility of dynamic aesthetic responses to the wonderland Americans inhabit."(Rolston III, 1986)

"Nature generates poetry, philosophy, and religion, and at its deepest educational capacity, Americans are awed and humbled by staring into the stormy surf of the midnight sky, by overlooking the canyon lands or by an overflight of migrating geese. If we must put it so, nature is a philosophical resource..."(Rolston III, 1986)

"The significance of nature is one of the richest assignments of mind, and this requires detection, imagination, participation, decision. The great outdoors works on a recreationist's soul, as well as on muscles and body."(Rolston III, 1986)

Productivity

"Recreation is big business. In 1984 Americans spent $262 billion on recreation and leisure, and $100 billion on outdoor recreation. Outdoor recreation, resources, facilities and activities generate economic activity. Some examples:

- The East Bay Regional Park District in California employs 300 permanent and 200 seasonal employees. The park system generates about $38.2 million (Gary Trudeau, East Bay Regional Park District)

- The total economic impact of over 11,000 organized recreation camps in the United States is over $2.5 billion (Armand Ball, American Camping Association)

- Ski areas produce a total revenue of $2.75 billion (Jim Branch, Sno-engineering, Inc.)

- A three-field softball complex in Lewiston, Maine with an initial cost of $150,000 added $160,000 to the local economy in just one year.

- Snowmobiling accounts for $1.3 billion in expenditures annually. Boaters spent $13.75 billion in 1985 for equipment and other needs. Fishermen spent $17.3 billion and hunters spent $8.5 billion in 1980 to pursue their sports. Whitewater rafting produces $60 million each year in Colorado alone. The annual sale of new recreational vehicles totals $6 billion. (PCAO *Recommendations*, 1986, p. 16

"Over the next 50 years the Chattahooche National Forest in northern Georgia will produce $108 million from timber and $637 million from recreation." (PCAO *Recommendations*, 1986, p. 17)

"The benefits to citizens of four urban parks in Worcester, Massachusetts, exceeded the annual operating costs by 4.5 to 1."(PCAO *Recommendations*, 1986, p. 17)

"In 1982, governments at all levels invested $8 billion in recreation and park programs, or $103 for every American household. Users of these government programs received total benefits of $26 billion, a benefit cost ration of 3:1."(PCAO *Recommendations*, 1986, p. 17)

"According to a 1986 Market Opinion Research Survey, three-fourths of American Adults traveled outside their communities to parks on all day trips. More than one-fourth (28%) of these adults visited park and recreation areas 10 or more times a year."(PCAO *Recommendations*, 1986, p. 17)

"It costs $30,000 a year to keep a kid in jail and many times they come out worse then when they went in. We are spending $3.33 a child per year for recreation and they are better for it."(PCAO *Recommendations*, 1986, p. 20)

"On average, the 50 state park systems last year recovered almost 40% of their $854 million operating costs through various fees, licensing and tax revenues, on-site sales and an assortment of other income producing devices."(Gimlin, 1988)

"Parkland is needed economically because industry benefits from the time and space parks provide for workers to recharge so they can stand up to competition of stronger international markets."(Hornback, 1989)

"Almost all institutions involved in the economic functions of production, consumption, accumulation and trade are potentially affected by recreation activities."(PCAO *Literature Review*, 1986)

3. What people say about Recreation and Parks

"Nearly 50% of Americans describe themselves as "outdoors people", and another 16% consider themselves a combination of indoors and outdoors people."(PCAO Recommendations, 1986, p. 8)

"Perhaps the biggest problem is that we take the outdoors for granted; we assume it will always be there, not recognizing that its maintenance depends on each of us." ((PCAO Recommendations, 1986, p. 9)

"In going outdoors I found I was only going home." John Muir

"Like winds and sunsets, wild things were taken for granted until progress began to do away with them." Aldo Leopold

"Wild animals are symbols of our nation. What effect would the extinction of the bald eagle--the symbol of our nation--have on American's optimism for our country's future? States adopt birds, flowers and trees that reflect their state's special identity. Natural symbols define America's tradition." (PCAO Recommendations, 1986, p. 19)

"The American adult public in early 1986 is in substantial agreement with these seven ideas which impact on what government policy should be with respect to outdoor recreation. The strength of agreement is greatest with the first idea and least with the last, but still the majority agreement crosses all demographic, geographic and motivational subgroups of the public."

- "The government should preserve natural areas for use by future generations."

- "Preservation of the natural environment is important for recreation."

- "More parks and recreation areas are needed near large cities."

- "The national government should continue to give financial assistance to local and state government for outdoor recreation."

- "I am willing to pay taxes which are dedicated to preserve natural areas of our country."

- "Local, state, or national government should provide access to beach and waterfront property on oceans, lakes, and rivers."

- "Maintaining the land and parks already available is more important than adding more parks." (Market Opinion Research, May, 1986)

"...If there is an overeaching goal for American recreation in the last year of this century, it is the frustratingly familiar but increasingly urgent challenge to balance the continuum of available recreation opportunities to achieve social, political, and economic justice for both the haves and have-nots of America, wherever this dichotomy appears or however it is defined."(Dunn, 1988)

4. The Status of Recreation and Parks

"Spending strictly for parks and recreation nationwide amounts to less than 1% of total annual government outlays."(PCAO Recommendations, 1986, p. 193

"When California lawmakers balked this year at approving a $776 million bond issue -- the biggest ever for outdoor recreation -- a strong network of park supporters...joining with the state's big tourist business and going over the legislators' heads by gathering enough petition signatures to put the issue directly before the electorate. In June's primary election the voters said yes by a large margin."(Gimlin, 1988, p. 58)

Participation

"Why Americans participate in outdoor recreation:(PCAO Recommendations, 1986, p. 25)

Enjoy/Enjoyment/Fun   36%

Exercise/Keep in shape   25%

To be outdoors?outside/Just to get out 22%

Health/Healthier/For the health/Feel good   15%

Fresh air   12%

"What American's do for outdoor recreation:(PCAO Recommendations, 1986, p. 26)

Walking for pleasure   84%

Driving for pleasure 77%

Sightseeing 77%

picnicking   76%

Swimming   76%

Visit zoos, fairs, amusement parks   72%

"Lifecycle determines how much time people spend on outdoor recreation. Young singles, young couples, and married couples with young children typically increase the time they spend in outdoor recreation. Those who have not changed or reduced the amount of time they spend include married couples with grown children, older singles and widows. Job pressures and health tend to reverse these trends. Children spend twice as much of their free time on recreation as adults."(PCAO Recommendations, 1986, p. 29)

"Since the 1960s three factors beyond population level, have significantly affected demand for outdoor recreation. These factors are leisure time, income, and mobility."

"*Leisure Time* -- we have experienced a decline in leisure time of about 8 hours per week since 1970. On the other hand, retirement is coming earlier for most Americans. Less than one out of four Americans waits until age 65 to retire."

"*Income* -- In 1985 the share of disposable personal income going to recreation was 6.4%. There is a significant public acceptance of user fees and charges at public recreation areas."

"*Mobility* -- Our freedom of movement expresses itself in our recreation choices as much as any other aspect of our lives. While the cross country auto trip was a common element in middle class America in years past, it has become less so in the past decade. This decline is reflected in fewer visits to remote areas of the National Park System, and is shown directly by the statistics on shorter recreation trips."(PCAO Recommendations, 1986, p. 33)

"Research overwhelmingly shows that family and home relationships, informal gatherings in public places, and mass recreation provide the leisure environment most people prefer." (Sapora, 1983)

"One expanding frontier that may still exist is related to people and their potential for developing social boundaries which depend only on creativity and productivity." (Sapora, 1983)

"Five types of motivations drive American adults to participate in outdoor recreation:

1. Fitness

    • For exercise

    • To keep healthy

    • To lose weight

    • To reduce stress

2   Social

- To have fun

- To be with friends

- For the family to be together

- For relaxation

3. Excitement

- For competition

- For excitement

- For risk and dancer

4. Experience Self and Nature

- To be alone

- To experience nature

5. Conformist/Space Cramped

- Because everyone else is doing it

- For space because home is cramped

"'The leisure ethic has become institutionalized in society."(Yankelovick, 1982). Employers are more sensitive to the leisure demands of workers as stress levels have risen for many in society."(Godbey, 1986)

Resources

"Here's what greenways can do for us and future generations:

- Provide Americans with access to open spaces and wildlands for the widest possible variety of outdoor activities, close to home;

- Conserve elements of the great American landscape, in all its diversity and the full potential for human interactions with that heritage;

- Build partnerships among private enterprise, landowners, and local governments and groups in recreation and conservation;

- Encourage local pride and celebration in the quality and availability of outdoor assets;

- Diversify and strengthen local economies and lifestyles through enhanced recreation opportunities;

- Link urban and rural areas for the recreation and conservation of natural resources."(PCAO Recommendations, 1986, p. 103)

"The growth of state park systems, especially parks, appears to have slowed dramatically in recent years. For example, state park systems gained 416,041 acres in 1979, including 403,965 acres by purchase. By 1983 state park acquisition had annually declined to 63,911 acres, with 18,307 acres acquired by purchase." (PCAO *Working Papers*, 1986,)

"The most frequently mentioned concern (48 states) was for establishment of <u>continuing, stable sources of funding</u> to support recreation programs:"

•   "'Rehabilitation, operation and maintenance' were the most frequently identified funding needs, followed closely by new development. More than half the states, however, cited major needs for protection of open space, natural lands, or historic areas that could involve funding of land acquisitions as one protection measure."

•   "Two thirds of state assessments say that federal matching funds for land acquisition, development, rehabilitation, and planning are essential components of continued, stable funding sources. Most praise the accomplishments of earlier federal recreation grant programs (LWCF and UPARR) and imply that these successful federal commitments have been curtailed prematurely."(PCAO *Working Papers,* 1986)

5.   Demand

"From the standpoint of need, it may be said that, while need for recreation is more abstract and lower on a hierarchy of need than for instance, need for food, a number of social Anthropologists have paid attention to recreation and play. Hall (1970) lists play as one of ten 'primary message systems' shared by all cultures. It has also been argued that periodic escape from stress and an over stimulating environment is essential to well-being."(Neal, 1983, p. 5)

"The 5,300 state operated parks and related facilities draw more than twice as many visitors as national parks, which tend to be far bigger, better known and stronger in public support."(Gimlin, 1988, p. 56)

"Overnight use of campgrounds, cabins, and lodges at state parks has increased faster than the overall surge in state park admissions during the past three decades. Overnight visits rose from 10 million to 15 million during the mid-1950s to 60 million last year, reflecting a rise in the affluence and outdoor interest of Americans."(Gimlin, 1988, p. 59)

"The changing preferences of our aging population from low cost, activity oriented recreation (picnicking, hiking, camping) to high cost, sedentary recreation (cabin and RV rental camping, travel to resort and commercial amusement destinations, outdoor recreation via cruises) will have an important consequence for park professionals."(Hornback, 1989, p. 36)

"As our society becomes older, better educated, and more economically constrained, the amount of participation in many forms of leisure activity may become less important than the quality of the experience. There is already some evidence that older people are highly sensitive to the qualitative aspects of recreation and park experiences such as level of maintenance, aesthetic considerations, and safety. The critical leisure consumer will increasingly seek high quality in both leisure products and leisure experience."(Godbey, 1986, Demand-6)

Bibliography

1. "American City and County Survey on Infrastructure Needs," (1988, November) *American City and County*.

2. Ball, Edith. (1983). In Neal, Larry L. (ed).*Leisure: No Enemy but ignorance.* Reston, VA: AAHPERD.

3. Brown, William E.(1971). *Islands of Hope.* Arlington, VA: National Recreation and Park Association.

4. Dunn, Diana. (1988). Goals for American recreation: An introduction. In Smith, S. Harold and Daniel D. McLean (eds.). *Leisure Today: Selected Readins IV*. Reston, VA: AAHPERD.

5. Gillespie, Glenn A. (Ed.). (1983). *Leisure 2000: Scenarios for the Future.* Columbia, MO: University of Missouri Press.

6. Gimlin, Hoyt. (1988, September) "What Covers 13 Million Acres, Sleeps 60 Million People and Desperately Needs Money?" *Governing the States and Localities.*, 1(12).

7. Godbey, Geoffrey. (1986). Some selected societal trends and their impact on Recreation and Leisure. In Literature Review, President's Commission on American's Outdoors. Washington, DC: US Government Printing Office.

8. Herbers, John. (1988, December)."For Captives of Federalism, It's Not Going to Get Better Soon," *Governing States and Localities.* 2 (3).

9. Hornback, Kenneth, (1989, April). "Leisure and Recreation Trends." *Leisure Today.*

10. *1988-The Municipal Yearbook.* (1988). Washington, DC: International City Managers Association.

11. *Journal of Physical Education, Recreation, and Dance.* (1983, September).

12. Market Opinion Research Corporation. (1986). Participation in outdoor recreation among American adults and the motivations which drive participation. In President' Commission on American's Outdoors, Working Papers. Washington, DC: US Government Printing Office.

13 Neal, Larry L. (Ed.). (1983). *Leisure: No Enemy but Ignorance.* Reston, VA: American Alliance for Health, Physical Education, Recreation, and Dance.

14. National Recreation and Park Association. (1984). *Demand for Recreation in America.* Alexandria, Va: National Recreation and Park Association.

15. President's Commission on American's Outdoors. (1986). *Case Studies..* Washington, D C: United States Government Printing Office.

16. President's Commission on American's Outdoors. (1986). *Literature Review.* Washington, D C: United States Government Printing Office.

17. President's Commission on American's Outdoors. (1986). *Recommendations*. Washington, D C: United States Government Printing Office.

18. President's Commission on American's Outdoors. (1986). *Working Papers*. Washington, D C: United States Government Printing Office.

19. Rolston, Holmes, III. (1986). Beyond Recreational Value: The greater outdoors preservation-related and environmental benefits. In President's Commission on American's Outdoors, *Literature Review*. Washington, DC: US Government Printing Office.

20 Sapora, Allen V. (1983).In Neal, Larry L. (ed).*Leisure: No Enemy but ignorance*. Reston, VA: AAHPERD.

21. Smith, S. Harold, and McLean, Daniel D. (Eds.). (1988). *Leisure Today: Selected Readings IV*. Reston, Va: American Alliance for Health, Physical Education, Recreation, and Dance.

22. The Academy of Leisure Sciences. (1983). *Values and Leisure and Trends in Leisure Services*. State College, PA: Venture Publishing.

23. The Council of State Governments. *The Book of the States, 1989-90*. (27), p. 523.

24. West, Patrick, C. (1986). Social benefits of outdoor recreation: Sociological perspectives and implications for planning and policy. In President's Commission on American's Outdoors, *Literature Review*. Washington, DC: US Government Printing Office.

NOTES

NOTES

NOTES

NOTES